DEEP BLUE FUNK

DEEP BLUE FUNK
& OTHER STORIES

Portraits of Teenage Parents

Daniel B. Frank

The Ounce of Prevention Fund
Chicago

The Ounce of Prevention Fund is a private, not-for-profit corporation jointly funded by the Illinois Department of Children and Family Services and the Pittway Corporation Charitable Foundation. The fund administers a unique statewide primary prevention program in Illinois. Six demonstration programs, designed to promote healthy family functioning, have been established. Through these programs comprehensive preventive health, educational, and social services are being offered to families at risk for child abuse and neglect. These model programs were developed to address problems related to the occurrence of child maltreatment. Such problems include teen pregnancy and parenting, low birth-weight infants, poor infant health, family isolation, and parental psychological problems related to self-esteem, ability to cope with stress, and lack of problem-solving skills. In addition, all programs include a rigorous ongoing evaluation designed to document the relationship between prevention efforts and reduction of parenting failures. The evaluation will also assess the impact and cost of such services.

One of the goals of the Ounce of Prevention Fund is the dissemination of knowledge related to clinical and research issues in a new and growing field. This book, as the first in a series of publications on primary prevention, represents an important step toward meeting that goal.

Published 1983
Printed in the United States of America

Library of Congress Cataloging in Publication Data

Frank, Daniel B.
    Deep blue funk and other stories.

    1. Adolescent parents—Illinois—Evanston. 2. Afro-American families—Illinois—Evanston. 3. Social work with youth—Illinois—Evanston. I. Title.
HQ759.64.F7   362.8'2   83-3965

For Pops and the Old Country,
in memory of Dr. Louis White,
my grandfather

Contents

Acknowledgments

Many people contributed to the making of this book. Most important are the young people and their families who shared with me part of their lives. Without their trust and friendship there would be no book. I also deeply appreciate the support of the men and women of the staff at Family Focus, Our Place. Working hard and with love, these adults know everyday how much adolescents want to be understood and accepted. For their special qualities, I want to thank: Freida Richmond, Ed Harrod, Diane Hibbler, Geneve Wade, Oneida Henry, Rudoll Carson, Art Pressley, Cathy Todd, Curtis Thomas, Val Adams and the members of the auxiliary board and Partners.

Irving B. Harris has an exceptional vision and a warm heart. It was his idea which lead me to write this book. I thank him for encouragement and support that is always gracious and loving. I am also indebted to Bernice Weissbourd, president of Family Focus, for her personal commitment to this book, and to Delores Holmes, director of Our Place, for her straightforward advice and valued trust. These three individuals, and the people with whom they work, demonstrate what is always possible to achieve, however modest and however local: social change.

Judith S. Musick, Ed Morris, and Katherine Downs, of the Ounce of Prevention Fund, and Katherine Kamiya Rubino deserve a most special thanks. I also thank Drue B. Cass, Stephanie Smith, and Joanne Goodman for typing and retyping various drafts of the manuscript.

Thomas J. Cottle provided me with invaluable advice at several points during the course of my research. I thank him, Barry O'Connell, Jan Dizard, and Bill Ray for their teaching and friendship.

This book has benefitted from the critical and creative suggestions offered by those individuals who read earlier drafts. With deepest gratitude I want to thank David R. Farber for his always daring thoughts and genuine friendship; Richard Locke for his tireless work and care; Joan W. Harris for her astute and attentive editorial judgment; and Gerald B. Frank for his journalist's eye.

Most especially, I thank Carol Levine, who knows so well what I think and how I feel, for her steady support, insight, and kind ways.

Preface

This is a story about children having children. *Deep
Blue Funk and Other Stories* is a book in which black
teenage parents speak for themselves about the lives
they lead as adolescents, as parents and expectant parents, as daughters and sons, as students, as hustlers, as
workers and jobless workers.

We hear much about the social, economic, and
psychological pressures under which American families live. We hear, as well, about teenagers who become
pregnant and have babies. Raising children, for parents
of any age, has its share of stress and strain. But teenagers who become parents experience a double pressure. They assume responsibility for the care and well-
being of a young, absolutely dependent human life at a
time in their own lives when they themselves are still
growing up.

The young people whose stories make up this book
tell of the difficulties they experience in their families
and in the families they have created. For many, becoming pregnant or fathering a child is the way they
have responded to the social and psychological pressures they feel.

These teens live in the predominantly black neighborhoods of Evanston, Illinois, the largely white,

affluent suburb immediately north of Chicago. Their stories are framed with the voices of their parents, grandparents, older friends, and relatives who told me how they feel about the effects of teenage pregnancy and parenthood. In addition, these adults talk about their fear of drugs, youth gangs, high school drop-outs, and adolescent suicide. All these, they believe, are related to the breakdown of the traditional lifelines of support that have existed in the black community: the church and the extended family.

Our Place is the name of the community center for teen parents and expectant parents where I met these young people and their families. I was hired by Family Focus, the social service agency that operates Our Place, to learn from these young people whether the center was providing real help to them. To carry out such an inquiry I felt I needed to spend more time at Our Place than a few interviews would allow. I wanted to establish my own relationships with the teens and not rely on a staff member who might ask for volunteers to come and talk to me. Together with the staff, I decided to create a position for myself at the center. I used my training and experience as a teacher to tutor kids with their school work or prepare them for the high school equivalency exam (GED). My role allowed me to work in the social science tradition of participant-observer. The conversations and observations I present reflect two years of friendships with these young people, their parents and families, the staff at Our Place, and a special group of adults who volunteer their time and energies at the center.

All of the people whose stories appear in this book knew before they talked to me that I might write about them. To assure confidentiality, I have changed all names except those of staff members at Our Place. Each person has read for accuracy in content and tone that section of the manuscript which pertains to him and has given permission to publish this work. In all cases it was I who requested the initial interviews. These conversations occurred in different settings and under many different circumstances. I did not use a tape recorder. I delayed all my notetaking until after a conversation had ended.

It did not take long to recognize that the scope of this project was larger than was originally intended, for I was not asking a specific set of questions in order to obtain measurable answers. As I talked and listened to these adolescents and adults, I began to hear much more than how they felt about their experiences at Our Place. I began to hear what they had to say about those matters which were important to them. I began to hear *how* they talked about their pasts, presents, and futures. And I heard what they had to say about their families and children, friends and neighbors, schools and churches, city and country. I heard about experiences shared with others and about experiences private and precious. I heard how they felt about me, a white, Jewish man, writing about them, young blacks.

I wanted to allow a group of young people, black teenage parents, so often talked about and "studied" by white adults, to speak for themselves, in their own words, about their lives. I guess there was something else I wanted. I wanted us to listen.

Who You Are, Where You Are, and What Time It Is

Pregnant girls stroll down Church Street. Young mothers push babies in strollers. Two-year-olds toddle at their mothers' heels. Church Street has a bad reputation. Good girls don't stand there. Their grandmothers told their mothers the same thing. Good boys, too, don't have time for Church Street. They play basketball or football or work or do their homework.

Stomachs round, backs arched, feet angled out toward the side, the girls walk slowly with a slight backward lean. Dressed in fashionable, freshly laundered clothes, they stroll east from the quiet tree-lined streets of their parents' five- or six-room working class bungalows, where the lawns are neatly mowed and the hedges are cut square and clean.

The intersection of Church and Dodge is an important corner in this neighborhood. Evanston Township High School, one of America's finest, dominates the block. Some of the girls who walk down Church Street, their young hands holding even younger hands, are enrolled there. Some will graduate. Too many will drop out. Across the street from the high school is a parking lot. Young men lean on parked cars and talk and sell dope. Splintered glass from broken wine bottles speckles the pavement. Cigarette butts lie at the foot of a parking meter where older men pass some time. Across the street from the parking lot is a drugstore, a small grocery store, and Doc's. Doc is eighty-two years old. He's been in Evanston since the Depression and still works. He sells candy, soda pop, notebooks, and pencils. He has a pay phone and four pinball machines. A sign posted on a glass counter top reads: "ATTENTION: Please do not put your shoes, luggage, radio, babies or any other items on the glass; it may break and injure someone." Kids are always in his store.

Next to Doc's is Our Place. Our Place starts off stark. A brick wall, a glass door, and two large picture windows make up the outside of this single-story, storefront building. A small recess leads to the front door. Kids stand there and talk and watch the street from its shadow. They smoke cigarettes. When they think no adults are around, they smoke reefer. In the heat of the summer, the smell of urine can be so strong that they have to find somewhere else to stand.

Inside, the hall shoots straight back from the front door. Alcoves and doors branch off on both sides. Some walls are wood paneled, but most are cement blocks covered with white ceramic tile. The space is divided into six main rooms: the parent room, childcare room, baby room, multipurpose room, the library, and the kitchen. There are four smaller spaces used for staff offices. The public health nurse uses one of these offices for an examining room. There are three bathrooms.

The kids and the staff have done a lot to brighten this simple space. Colorful signs, posters, and drawings follow the length of the hall and adorn the walls in each room. To the left of the front door is a large bulletin board. On the board is a display, decorated with blue and white construction paper. Twenty-six white storks fly among white clouds in a blue sky. Each stork carries a diaper in its long beak. In each diaper is a brown card on which is the name of a child newly born to one of the girls who uses the center. A sign written in red magic marker reads, "WELCOME TO THE WORLD! WELCOME TO OUR PLACE!"

To the right of the door another sign reads:

Please Check
Your hat + cap
Here, House rules
Thank You—

Farther down the hall is a table where there is a pile of the center's monthly calendar of activities, events, and services. An announcement of job notices and employment workshops lies next to the calendar. A clipboard and pen sit in the center of the table. On the clipboard are several sheets of paper on which all those who enter sign their names. Another house rule. Names fill the pages. About fifty a day. Some are given names. Some are nicknames. Others appear to be self-assigned aliases. The names and ages of the babies and young children also appear on these sheets. About ten a day.

Above the table hangs a poster with a photograph of a teenage boy holding a baby's bottle. He is testing the temperature of the milk by shaking the bottle so that the milk will hit his wrist. Above the boy's head is a clock. It's two o'clock. A baby's crib lies off to the right. Words are printed at the bottom of the poster:

Jimmy used to think a 2:00 A.M. feeding was a late night pizza.

Find out the facts of life before experience becomes the worst teacher.

Beyond the poster is a door. The door is covered entirely with a brilliant yellow paper. A small square has been cut out for the doorknob. At eye level is a red heart bordered by a purple leaf. On the heart, in black type, is a prayer posted by a member of the staff after a young mother died of hemorrhage only hours after she had given birth to a baby boy:

Dear Lord, Almighty Father: You are the ruler of the heavens and the earth; your son is Jesus Christ and Savior of all our souls; your Holy Spirit is everlasting. Please help me to better my condition on this earth. Don't let me live in the past; let me live for today and many tomorrows. Let my years be prosperous.

Don't let hate and jealousy and fear linger in my heart, only love and compassion. Don't let sickness invade my body and mind, only good health and strength, and let my faith be strong. Let my mind go as high as the highest mountain and from these elevate to the skies, to the heavens from which you look down upon us. Let me not dwell upon the lowly things for I will soon become as one of them. This prayer I write in all sincerity and I hope that you hear and answer it.

Amen

A large plant sits by the door to the baby room. Above the plant are two collages, mosaics of magazine photographs and headlines. All photographs are of children. Some photographs are of children and adults. All photographs are of black faces. A headline reads, "Caring Is Everything."

A table stands next to a large magazine rack. On the table leaflets and literature on a variety of health matters speak their message:

Smoking: So You Want to Stop

Facts on Breast Cancer

Life Insurance: A Buyer's Guide

Rape: Be Aware

Diaphragms

Beginnings: Discussions of Pregnancy and Parenthood

No! And Other Methods of Birth Control

Food before Six: A Feeding Guide for Parents of Young Children

Opposite the table is another bulletin board: job notices, newspaper clippings, announcements of local community events, invitations to baby showers.

The parent room faces Church Street. The kids like this room most. It is the only room with windows. A sun shade covers the two picture windows, making them one-way mirrors: the teens can watch Church Street, but Church Street can't watch them. Two black couches, one vinyl, one leather, a love seat and an assortment of folding chairs line the walls. A rust-colored carpet covers the floor. Three sewing machines sit on a long table. A gallery of the teens' drawings, paintings, and collages are mounted on the wood-paneled walls. Despite staff efforts to encourage the teens to use the other rooms more often, the kids still drift back to the parent room. It's their living room. They like the window.

The multipurpose room is the largest room. Ping pong, dancercise, meetings, Wednesday night dinners, Thursday afternoon movies take place here. As in the hall, posters and photographs of famous black men and women, both African and American, are taped to the walls: Monsa Konkon, king of Mali; Hannibal, ruler of Carthage; Rev. Dr. Martin Luther King, Jr.; Jean Baptiste Point du Sable, Chicago's first settler; Charolette Fortea, teacher, poet, author; A. Philip Randolph, labor leader, civil rights activist; Thurgood Marshall, Supreme Court justice. A hall of fame. Face to face: African and American experiences; African warriors and American survivors.

The library is warm and simple: a small couch, two bookcases, a magazine rack, a table in the center of the room, four chairs surrounding the table. One bookcase houses a ready supply of board games and puzzles: Downfall, Stay Alive, The Rescuers, The Black Experience. Books line the other set of shelves: elementary school arithmetic, grades four, five and six; a text on citizenship and an encyclopedia; sports books; books on Africa, American Slavery, Harlem Renaissance, Black Power; GED preparation books; a few dictionaries; books on occupation and career choice. The board game Sorry lies on top of this bookcase.

Cribs and baby toys take up most of the baby room. A rocking chair stands in the corner. The floor is carpeted. This room shares a common door with the child-care room, a room with shelves of toys, wall drawings of smiling brown bears holding little green bears, yellow rabbits leaning against white clouds, and baby skunks with delightful grins sniffing flowers. A tank of gold fish sits on a table. Photographs framed by a young mother hang near the door. Charts of information about child safety and child development are posted about the room.

Our Place was named by a tough sixteen-year-old mother nicknamed "Cookie." Our Place is where Cookie and other teens hang out, get off the streets, spend some time talking with friends and staff about those matters that concern them. Our Place is where Geneve Wade, a creative young woman raised in Evanston, helps the girls make their own dresses. She designs her own clothes and brings in colorful fabrics and patterns in the latest style. Diane Hibbler, another Evanstonian and mother of two teenage boys, sits on the floor and plays with the babies and talks to the young mothers about child development. When she first came to work at Our Place, Diane was shocked by the teenagers' dirty language. She was also surprised at the fathers' interest in their babies. After three years, Diane knows that young mothers will come to her feeling upset when their babies won't stop crying or when their toddlers won't be toilet trained in one night. Girls tell her, "I wish you were my mother"; and girls get angry at her because she can't be fooled. She knows what kind of care they give their babies.

Young men come to play ping pong and to talk to Ed Harrod about some problems. Ed wears a cap and has a mean passion for jazz. He laughs when the teens call jazz "old fogey" music. He's a St. Louis man who can't get his home town out of his blood. Ed talks to the guys about fatherhood, relationships, work, school, and responsibility. He coaches their basketball team. He asks the fathers to follow his example and take their hats off when they are inside the center. They know he takes them seriously. He knows what they're up against. Oneida Henry is known to the teens as Mother Henry. She speaks softly and has twelve children of her own. She can make a meal out of nothing. Teens and their children often come to her hungry, looking for something to eat. Cathy Todd is a nurse from Evanston's Public Health Department who is assigned to work at Our Place several days a week. She's usually the first to know. She runs the pregnancy tests. She cringes as she hears girls make plans to celebrate when their test results come back positive. She says, "From a teen's point of view, the problem isn't getting pregnant, it's *not* getting pregnant." She also hands out birth control devices, hears confessions, and counsels girls about venereal disease and prenatal care.

Freida Richmond has a warm smile and a gentle manner. She touches the teens. She says, "They need to *feel* we care." Pregnant girls, boys who are fathers, and their families—Freida talks and listens to them at the center and at church, in their homes and on the phone, late at night. She hears their troubles and looks for their strengths. Gang members and black ministers know Freida. She organizes community meetings in local churches and talks tough to school administrators. She's worried about the future of Evanston's black youth; she's worried about drugs and she's worried about gangs. She's worried that the teens will have to move out of Evanston to the north side of Chicago because there is not enough low income rental housing in Evanston to accommodate them. Freida's angry that the parks do not have enough supervised summer activities for children and teenagers. She's angry that Evanston Township High School isn't more responsive to those students who want vocational training instead of college prep. Some people say she's a radical; she says, "I'm just trying to get things done." Eating peanuts and smoking cigarettes keep her going through the day.

Five days a week the center is open for teen parents, twice a week for teens who are not parents. Family Focus intended the center only for teen parents and their children. But when the doors first opened, crowds of curious youth walked in, many of whom were not parents. For them, the center was a new place in the neighborhood for kids, and the staff did not want them to think they had to get pregnant and have babies in order to spend time at Our Place. Workshops and rap groups run nearly every day. Kids and staff talk about sexuality, budgeting, racism, nutrition, fatherhood, post-partum blues. Counseling takes place by appointment or as a casual talk in a corner. Once a week a group called Partners meets. This group is made up of teen mothers and adult women who had become mothers when they were teenagers. Each teen has a senior partner she visits or talks to by phone at least once a week.

That Our Place is on Church Street is no accident. It's close to the high school and in the heart of the black community, the area of the highest number of teenage mothers. Community leaders, black and white, thought it would be a good idea. The City of Evanston even came up with $50,000 to help buy the building.

It all sounds so simple. A casual place for teen parents to talk and feel good about themselves. But let's not forget. Sex is why Our Place exists. Sex is why kids come to Our Place.

A girl laughs with a friend who wears a t-shirt that reads, "If You Think Sex Is a Pain in the Ass, You're Doing It Wrong!" A boy plays to a girl he might know, "Hey, hey, baby, all you got to do is put it up." Three girls giggle when one holds up a two-foot-long papier maché peanut and says, "If I saw one that size, I'd run!" Another says, "Shoot, I bet if you saw one that size, you'd take it on all the way!"

Sex is a language of life. Over twelve million American teenagers are sexually active; more than a million girls become pregnant each year. In 1978, 434,000 girls had abortions, 554,000 gave birth, and 362,000 gave birth out of wedlock. Each year, four out of ten girls will get pregnant. Two out of ten will give birth.*

White girls in Evanston get pregnant, but if they do they almost always have abortions. Most black girls in Evanston don't believe in that. Religious convictions run strong in this community among young and old, and abortions are expensive. Giving up babies for adoption outside the extended family is almost never done. But religious convictions, financial restraints, and resistance to adoption are not the causes of teenage parenthood.

Casual sex hardly has casual consequences for these or any other teen parents. For them sex results in unanticipated and awesome changes in their young lives. Too late they learn that being a parent is different from being pregnant. Feelings change; the reality only

Teenage Pregnancy: The Problem That Hasn't Gone Away (New York: Alan Guttmacher Institute, 1981).

becomes clear upon giving birth. Being pregnant means being the center of attention, wanting to keep a boyfriend, or wanting to create something special. Getting a girl pregnant is often an attempt to prove to peers and parents that one is now a man. Becoming a parent, however, means sharing or even losing that center-stage spotlight to the baby; it means being a mother when one still needs to be mothered; it means discovering one's lack of the financial and emotional resources to live up to the vision of what a "real" man, a "real" father does. A teenager wants to have a baby in order to feel important and dignified, to feel good about herself because she has not felt good enough before. Becoming a parent is an attempt to secure intimacy, love, and safety, to claim identity and a new status. Or, it may be an attempt to save one's family from violence, separation, or divorce by creating a crisis around which the whole family must unite.

And yet, for some adults in the black community of Evanston, teenage sex, pregnancy, and parenthood are really not the worst concerns. Many are more frightened of drugs and gangs than they are of pregnancy and parenthood. One woman put it to me this way: "We've been having families and children for a long time now. Sure it's hard on everyone to have a little girl have a baby of her own. There's no denying that. It creates all kinds of trouble in the family. But one way or another we can take that little baby on. Somehow the family becomes big enough. But with drugs, and I don't mean just reefer, and gangs, well, that's a different story. They make our kids crazy, and we're losing them."

Fear of losing a generation of children motivates the adults to organize their community. They want to talk and listen to each other: parents to children, clergy to congregation, neighbor to neighbor. Their goal is to strengthen the bonds of the extended family: relatives, friends, and neighbors. In community meetings held at Our Place and in the basements of local churches, adult parents talk about teenage pregnancy and parenthood. But they are also talking about relationships between adult men and women, gangs, family abuse, religion, political awareness, education, and child development. Our Place serves as the catalyst for most of this discussion and organizing because it has come to be a symbol of autonomy and survival for an economically fragile black community, an island-ghetto in an affluent white suburb. One woman, a mother of three boys, said this at a community meeting: "If our children are droppin' out, drugged out, ganged out, knocked up and havin' babies, or coppin' out altogether, you tell me what kind of shape they're going to be in to take on all we've made for our people here in Evanston." To lose a generation of its youth, even part of it, would mean to lose what it took generations to get: a slice of the pie.

In a community where not everyone is sympathetic to those teens who are having babies, who are joining gangs, or who are using drugs, the staff at Our Place provides friendship and support. An elderly woman said to Freida Richmond on a Sunday after church: "Look at all these kids. It's disgusting, all the drug-dealing and gang activities that's going on. And all these young girls walking around pregnant or with their little children. I tell you, it ain't safe for old people in this town no more. We should clean'em off the streets. That's right, just mow'em down and kill'em."

I heard Freida reply, "You'll be going to an awful lot

of funerals of your friends' kids and grandkids. All these kids, even the ones you see on Church Street, all live somewhere. They all have families. They're not from Mars. These are our kids. They only live down the block or around the corner."

When I began my work at Our Place, I was given a piece of advice by Delores Holmes, director of the center. "Be patient," she said. "Pay attention to the kids and their needs. Watch what they're doing and listen to what they say. Forget about your book. Forget about your interviewing and writing. If you can do that, you'll have a chance at winning their trust and hearing what they're about."

One afternoon, in my first month at Our Place, I was standing on the corner of Church and Dodge talking with Freida. A young mother ran to us from across the street. She was smiling and talking excitedly. She reached into her purse and handed to Freida, and then to me, two color photographs of a baby girl about three months old. It was her baby. The girl seemed so happy, so proud to show us her photographs. "Isn't she pretty?" the girl said. I stood there, moved by the feeling between Freida and this young mother. After a few minutes, the girl put her photographs back in her purse. She gave Freida a quick hug, smiled, and ran back across the street. Freida then turned to me. "Oh, Dan, that poor girl is carrying on as if her baby were still alive. That baby died over three months ago." Show and tell on the street corner.

At a community conference called "Helping Youth through Families," sponsored by Our Place, I stood with a sixteen-year-old boy at the back of the room.

The conference speakers, two local school officials and a dean from Northwestern University, addressed the seated gathering of eighty adults and seven teenagers. Throughout the speeches I found myself listening to two people at once. With one ear I listened to the notable adults; with the other I listened to my sixteen-year-old friend, Isaac Washington, give a running commentary on what he heard.

A speaker said,"We must become more involved with our children. We must provide our kids with positive role models. We must keep our eyes and ears open to what may be troubling a child. We must not neglect our children by allowing them to do poorly in school, to be disrespectful to their elders, to be disillusioned with themselves. All children need love, acceptance, encouragement, and self-confidence. The time to act is now, the time for parents to assert themselves for their children is always now."

Meanwhile, Isaac, his head cocked toward mine, spoke to me in a low tone out of the side of his mouth. "Would you listen to this superficial shit. I mean, I know they mean well 'n all, but they're talking about symptoms and not problems. They can talk all they want to about saving children, but that's a long way from doing something about it, and I mean major. . . . I heard this lady, man, a school teacher, mind you, one of the great child-savers, say that psychiatrists just give kids excuses for their problems. Take some of these kids around here, the ones that are in the gangs, for example. They're not just a bunch of low-down, dumb kids. They're just people with problems.

"Listen to this guy. Is he telling us why kids have problems? No, not really. Just the same old words:

love, support, help, care, attention. The problems I'm
thinkin' of are a matter of life and death. He's not
telling us that kids try and kill themselves. Lord help
these well-meaning adults. I wonder if they really know
what kids are like. You ever notice how many kids play
those video games? Video games are a kid's salvation.
It's meditation, man. It's how I get my frustrations
out. It's generational war against your parents. Just
blow'em up and die, die, die, and never live again. . . .
My grandfather's always giving me his "kids today"
speech. He says kids don't give a shit about work and
planning ahead for the future. He says it's 'cause we
don't have any religion and belief in God. Now that
stuff is real bullshit. Pure brainwashing. Don't mix
reality and religion with me. I got plenty of reasons why
I *know* there's no God. If there was a God he wouldn't
make kids suffer. If he was any kind of good God he
wouldn't put kids in horrible situations which make
them want to kill themselves. I know, I tried once. My
parents had gotten divorced and I was caught in the ol'
double whammy. One day I just had enough. I layed
down by the gas fireplace and turned it on. The gas
made me fall asleep and I started to dream. I dreamt I
was standing on a hill over a valley and on the other side
I saw my other self. The other me was screaming,
'C'mon over here you sonofabitch! You fuckin' sissyass
wimp! C'mon, faggot face, c'mon over here!' I was
freaking out, man, 'cause I didn't want to go, I just
didn't want to. I wasn't ready to die. It wasn't my
time."

As Isaac continued to talk, I heard Dean Jenkins, of
Northwestern, speak. "Young people suffer because of
miscommunication among adults and between adults

and kids. Kids need strength and wisdom to grow up. And the wisdom needed for growing up lies in the pursuit of answers to three problems: Who you are, where you are, and what time it is."

Sighing softly, Isaac spoke again. "Yeah," he said in a reflective tone. "Who you are, where you are, and what time it is. Now that cat's got it, man." Isaac smiled for the first time that morning.

Freida Richmond and Isaac Washington are only two of the people I came to know during the time I spent at Our Place. On the pages that follow, you will hear the voices of many other young people and adults who were generous and trusting enough to allow me to share a part of their lives.

A Preacher's Warning

I

"Lord have mercy!"

Four bodies turn. Four pregnant girls look out a large picture window onto Church Street.

"Would you look at that?" the same voice exclaims. The girl points to a crowd of friends across the street. I look, too.

Two more girls race to the window. Some girls lean so close to the window, straining to observe every detail, that they rustle the sun screen that keeps the hot summer sun out of the parents' room.

I remain seated on the couch and watch the girls watch their friends. All eyes fasten on the scene across the street. The sun shade is perfect. A one-way mirror, to see but not be seen. Spying is fun.

"Now, ain't that the same Laura Williams that was up in here about two weeks ago?" the girl continues.

"Sure is."

"Look at that girl, would you! Walkin' around in those tight jeans and that t-shirt all tucked up real tight around her belly," says another girl.

"And you *know* what she's tryin' to show off, too, don't you," continues a friend leaning over her shoulder.

"I heard that!" blurts another. "She was in here not too long ago wearin' these baggy ol' pants and a big ol' sweatshirt."

"You know somethin's comin' down. That girl's got herself pregnant and wants the whole world to know her business," rings out one more voice.

"She'll find out soon enough that belly she's paradin' around is gonna get mighty uncomfortable when she gets to be my size," says a young mother-to-be in her eighth month. "I feel all bloated. My legs ache and my back's been killin' me for a week. I'll be feelin' much better once I have my baby." She rests her hand on the small of her back.

"You never know," muses a girl who appears to be near her sixth month, "ol' Laura over there could be actin' the way this one girl I know was. This girl had all the right signs of bein' six months gone: no period, her breasts were all swollen, and she had a big ol' belly. The whole bit. Then this doctor tells her she ain't pregnant at all. She wanted to get pregnant so bad she had got herself pregnant. It was all in her head. Dig that; she had all the right signs, but wasn't pregnant at all!"

"Yeah, but you sure got more than just signs there, honey!" a voice fires back sending everyone into hysterics.

Three more teens walk into Our Place and move toward the parent's room. They are met by Ed, a staff member. They know already what he's going to say; they've heard it many times.

Ed reminds the girls that today is Tuesday, and the center is open only for teen parents. None of them is pregnant or a parent. All they hear is: "Get out." Obviously angered, one of the girls explodes, "What is it about this place? Do I have t'a go out 'n get pregnant to come up in here?"

Rita is eighteen and has a fifteen-month-old daughter. She winces as she hears the girl speak. "When are those girls ever gonna get it straight," she says. "This place is good and all, but it sure ain't worth gettin' pregnant just to hang out here in the afternoons. Just quit bein' crazy, girl."

"Aw, don't worry 'bout it, Rita. I'm not *that* stupid," the girl replies. "I ain't gonna have no babies 'til I'm older and married at that."

"Don't be so sure of yourself, honey. I thought the same thing about a year ago. A girl's got to watch herself *real* close. Don't be deceivin' yourself about how wonderful havin' a baby is . . . and how sweet some little boy is to you. Just don't be so sure of yourself!"

Rita is shaken by the vehemence of her speech. She walks back to where she has been sitting. Her daughter, Kimberly, watches her mother from across the room. Sensing her mother's mood, she waddles over and holds on to her yellow print skirt.

"Get your dirty hands off me, girl!" Rita commands her wide-eyed daughter. "What do you think you're doin' messin' up my clean skirt, huh?" Rita continues to ignore her daughter and the attention her daughter seeks from her. "You know, I should have given you up when I had the chance," she says as she strikes a match and lights a cigarette.

"I always *did* want that baby," another mother says in a tone that is both sarcastic and serious.

"Yeah, Rita, you've sure got one short memory," another girl teases in agreement. "You remember when you wanted to give away Kimberly the last time, about a year ago? And she went and stayed with her father for three or four days? Oh, girl. You came back so fast, crying . . . 'Please, oh, please, I want my baby back, I want my Kimberly back!' " Rita's tight expression eases and a crack in her smile breaks into a laugh. Yet despite the softening of her tense posture, Rita still doesn't want to pick up her daughter, who remains leaning against her legs. Another mother reaches out and picks up Kimberly to cuddle her.

"Hey, that's all right sweet lady," she tells Kimberly. "We ain't gonna let you or your mother wig out on us."

The room becomes still. The cigarette smoke rises. A mother wipes the corners of her baby's mouth. A baby lies on the couch sucking his bottle. Another mother withdraws into her own quiet with her baby on her stomach and her thumb in her mouth.

"Would you look at that little face just smiling away," sighs a young mother as she feeds her four-month-old son. "Isn't he just something, smiling with his big ol' eyes!"

"Well, if it was me bein' fed and I had to look up at you, I'd be screaming!" cracks a girl from across the room, breaking everyone up.

"You know, you're lucky you had a boy," says Leona, a heavy-set, big-breasted girl. "I'm going on eight months and I hope to Jesus he's a boy. Girls cause too much trouble. Look at most of us and you'll see what I mean. Us girls, we're evil sometimes. And rebellious, too, honey. And it only gets us into trouble in the end. All my sisters had boys and they're easy. Little boys don't give you a hard time. If you say sit, they sit. 'Cause little boys is always scared of their mothers."

"Listen, Leona," Rita replies, "don't you go ideal-

izin' the mens around here. They may be easy to man-
age when they're little, but they're just as mean and as
bad as us when they get older. If not more. You know
damn well they're some dudes around here who think
nothin' of beatin' on their women. They think it's their
right. Believe me, girl, I know."

Rochelle, an eighteen-year-old, sits by the door. She
wears a light blue neatly tailored summer pants suit, a
white cotton blouse and white plastic sandals. She
seems to like the way she looks. Rochelle sits cross-
legged and swings her foot slightly as she listens to the
others speak. When not intermittently biting a fingernail, her mouth is closed tightly. Her brown eyes look
toward the floor and her eyebrows are drawn together.
She listens closely to Leona's and Rita's exchange.

"You know," Rochelle finally says, "you all should
be just grateful that your babies are healthy, regardless
of what sex they is. I just get sick and tired of hearing
some of you bitch about your kids and all your responsibilities. You all shouldn't be havin' no kids if you ain't
prepared to raise'em right and love'em. You just don't
know how lucky you all is." She turns her eyes to Leona
and then to Rita. "Man, if I had a baby I'd love it so
much, boy or girl. There wouldn't be anything I
wouldn't do for my baby."

She pauses.

"But I wasn't one of the lucky ones. I lost my two
babies. They both died."

II

Rochelle comes to Our Place for GED tutoring
about twice a week. We work at a table in the library.
We have met regularly for nearly five months.

One afternoon, after about forty-five minutes of

study, one of the other girls brings each of us a cup of baked beans, courtesy of the girls in the cooking class.

"It's good somebody likes those things," Rochelle says with a grimace. "You won't get me eatin' no nasty beans. Oooo, I hate beans. I had to eat them for about two weeks straight in this home I had to live in once for girls who were, you know, in trouble. That's all they'd serve you at this place was nasty ol' beans. Beans, beans, beans, morning, noon, and night. So when I see beans now it just reminds me of that wicked ol' place. That was a while ago, anyhow, when I was runnin' away a lot, 'round when I was fourteen or so. Just too many family problems, if you know what I mean. Shit, just to keep my sanity I had to get away from there. And that's partly why I never finished high school. I was just runnin' too damn much."

She watches me eat.

"You know, Dan, it feels good to be working and studying like this. I feel as if I'm doin' somethin' that's gonna be good for me. That's one thing I can always say about myself, that I ain't afraid to work and that I ain't never been on welfare."

She leans forward in her chair, propping an elbow on the table and pointing a finger at me as if she were making a speech. "No way would I ever go on welfare, even if my baby hadn't a died I wouldn't have gone on welfare. That would have been a more responsible thing to do. Least I'd a been supportin' myself and workin'.

"If you can work, I think you should. It's just too damn bad it's so hard to get a job these days, particularly with Reagan and all these damn cutbacks. That shit is really gonna hurt a lot of black families, I tell you, and a lot of white families, too, at that. And it's not that I'm picky or anything, I ain't stubborn like some people I know who won't work unless they're makin' some down money. The way I look at it is that you've got to start somewhere. Hell, I'd even be a maid for a while. There's things I want to do in this world and I got to have money to do it with.

"I'll tell you one thing, I sure don't agree with them who say that the government owes me this and the government owes me that. Shoot, I just want to work, plain and simple. And let me tell you something else, too," she says looking me in the eye as her voice becomes louder and more determined, "even when I was younger, around when I was fourteen and fifteen and sixteen, and getting into all sorts of trouble runnin' away and shit, I always had a job. If it wasn't at Burger King, or if it wasn't Kentucky Fried Chicken, it was somewhere. I always had a job. Because I had to have a job."

She pounds her fist on the table. She takes a long drag from her cigarette. Her eyes squint as they follow the upward path of the smoke. She places the cigarette on the lip of the ashtray.

"You know, Dan, I'm tryin' real hard to get myself together. I want to get myself a good job someday, one that makes good money and that's got some security. I don't want to become super rich or nothing. Just, you know, comfortable. I want to be able to live without worryin' so that someday I can support myself and my children. That's why I'm goin' back to this school.

"Sometimes I feel real good about myself tryin' to reach these goals, other times I get depressed about it. I look back on my past and think of all that went wrong

and feel like there's too much for me to overcome."
She bites a fingernail. "Maybe it's good for me to look
at my past and understand it. But mainly I just want to
forget it, just erase it from the blackboard in my mind.

"I can sit here and think about what it was like to be
in school and how I oughtta have stayed and finished
high school instead of droppin' out when I was a sopho-
more, and thinkin' that if I had only stayed in there my
life would be a lot easier. Sometimes when I think
about the past I only remember the good parts, or at
least those parts that weren't so bad. Then there's other
times when I hear some kind of devil talking in my ear,
'You should a done this or you should a done that.'
'Thanks a lot!' is what I feel like sayin', what good is
knowin' that now? Someone should a told me then that
somethin' bad was gonna happen. But really, I think I
would've finished high school all right if I just hadn't
had so much on my mind at the time. Part of me always
liked school. I got a quick mind for things, but I also got
a quick tongue and that always got me in trouble. Back
in sixth or seventh grade I started learnin' that I was
different than a lot of other people; I mean, I wouldn't
just sit quiet if I thought somethin' was wrong or unfair.
Maybe 'cause at the time I was the only black kid in this
private school I had went to. I don't know. I'd just
speak my mind. And doin' just that got me thrown out
of school once in eighth grade. I tell you, I went wild in
those years. I was even cussin' teachers out." She
smiles mischievously.

"And by the time I was enterin' high school, things at
home were just so messed up that it was really gettin' to
me. My mother was always arguin' with my father
about money 'cause he wouldn't give her no child sup-

port and made my mother have to work harder and longer hours. It was scandalous. Just thinking of my father, my so-called father, makes me so mad."

She looks at me out of the corner of her eye. "He still doesn't give us a dimes' worth of support, but he still thinks he's got parental rights. He left us when I was five years old and damn near abandoned us except when my mother felt like she couldn't handle me. Then she'd send for him to come over and whup me, sayin' bullshit like 'father knows best.' But I just said no way, 'you must think I'm so dumb to think you can scare me.' No way.

"I remember this one time he came over with his big ol' belt and I tore outta that house and ran down the street. Boy was I fast! I'd be cussin' him out and he'd be chasin' me! This one time this girl friend of mine was runnin' with me and we hid in these bushes. I saw the buckle on his belt shine from the reflection of the streetlight. I told my girlfriend, 'Don't breathe.' Oh, boy, our lungs were heaving in and out so hard! It was a total trip!" She blows her lungs in and out demonstrating for me how her lungs billowed that night.

"But soon the chasing routine was makin' me real sick. So I started to run away even more. Nowhere too special at first. Just down the block to a girl friend's house. It wasn't like *really* running away, but it was all I could do. Sometimes I'd stay away for a month or more, and after a while my mother just gave up and didn't even try to find out where I was. Things got real bad when my mother started working at night and my older sister started playing bossy mother. Shit, she was awful. I couldn't do nothin' without her permission. Tellin' me when I could go to the bathroom and when I couldn't. Orderin' me around like she was our mother or somethin'. And she'd be hittin' us, too.

"The thing was, I wasn't real afraid about runnin' away and being put in no Audy home. You see, I figured my mother out pretty well. I figured she wouldn't let me go to no Audy home 'cause that would reflect back on her that she was a bad mother. And she was worryin' 'bout so much then that she wouldn't want to have to think that she was a bad mother on top of all that, too."

She takes another long drag on her cigarette.

"So between all this yellin' and threatenin' and hittin' at home and my troubles with them girls up there at that high school, I was gettin' real upset. It would really upset me when some of those girls would get so jealous of me 'cause I could talk to people easily, especially the guys, and 'cause I dressed nice and I had nice hair. They really hated me 'cause some of their boyfriends like me and then they'd say I gave them the wrong eye or something and then they'd want to fight me. I bet you didn't think girls liked to fight, did you? Well, they do. And I knew they was gonna pick on me, 'cause I was the smallest, and they always be pickin' on the smallest person.

"And besides, my father wasn't givin' me or any of my sisters and brothers any money. My mother didn't have anything to give me for books when I started high school. I figured if I didn't have any books what was the damn use of going to classes. And since I was missin' so many classes, the school put me in some kind of special classes, which were actually okay. They was smaller than regular classes and that was much better for me.

Havin' less students around meant I could get more of the teacher's attention."

She leans back in her chair, her eyes look into her lap. "I think I'm different than a lot of people. Sometimes I feel real old and real tired, like I'm an old person or something. I guess part of that is I'm a loner, sort of. I mean, I've got friends and all, but down deep I think I'm a loner. And that brings me down. There's just too much gossip and too much jealousy around here for me. I just don't respect that shit. My values are real different than some of these girls who come up in here gossipin' all day about this girl or that boy. Sometimes I just don't understand why people can't just love each other like they're supposed to." Her eyes look at me almost asking for an answer. "And this morning, my mother starts comparin' me to these other people. But if she only knew the real truth; that only kids can know who should be compared to who. 'Cause we're all hangin' together. Just think," she says, shaking her head, "the ones she was comparin' me to is really a couple of jerks."

Rochelle rises from the table, gathers her papers and books and piles them neatly next to her purse. The book which sits on top of this pile is titled *Nobody Is Listening to Me.*

She puts on her long brown coat and places a blue knitted hat on her head. It is five o'clock and she is ready to pick up her young nephew, James, from day care and cook dinner for him as she does nearly every night.

"I tell you, Dan, it just isn't fair. My mother should be tryin' to help me by tellin' me that it's good that I'm tryin' to get myself together and that she's proud of me. But I'm still treated like the black sheep of the family."

As Rochelle speaks, I am not looking at her, although she is looking at me. Instead my eyes focus on the title of her book.

"That's one reason why I like kids so much," she says, "and why I liked working with them at the day-care center after my baby died. I can identify with them. Many of the little kids I know is worse off than I was and I don't want any of them little angels to go through what I've gone through. That's why I hate parents who abuse their children. Little kids can be oppressed so easily. I grew up in a house where children 'were to be seen and not heard' and that's probably why I had to scream and carry on the way I did, to get someone's attention to notice me, to take me seriously.

"It was like feeling as if I wasn't important to the people I should be important to. I was feelin' as if I wasn't loved by the people who I loved and who should have loved me. And without that kind of equality, you just can't have any happiness or love. And that's a kind of oppression, too, isn't it, Dan?"

III

I continue to work and talk with Rochelle, but she has begun to miss our tutoring appointments. We have seen each other only twice in nearly eight weeks. Sometimes Rochelle offers reasons why she doesn't come, sometimes she simply doesn't.

Her repeated absences puzzle me. Why does she arrange to meet me and then not show up? I am beginning to feel impatient and frustrated. "How's Wednesday at three o'clock?" she'd suggest. "That's fine," I'd reply. "I'll see you then." And how many Wednesdays have I had to cool my heels waiting for Rochelle?

One Wednesday, tired of waiting and realizing that Rochelle was not going to meet me as we had planned, I decide to walk the three blocks to her house to see if she is home.

Frances Lawson answers the door and invites me into her living room. Although we have met before, I am struck again by how little Rochelle resembles her mother. Rochelle is small-boned, thin, and dark-skinned. Her mother is big-boned, large, and light-skinned. At a glance one would hardly guess that they are mother and daughter. I explain to her that I am looking for Rochelle and voice my concern that she has missed several meetings with me. Mrs. Lawson looks exasperated and worried.

Mrs. Lawson sits at the dining room table, her hands folded in front of her. I sit on a couch across from her. "I don't know what's going on with that girl, she can't keep her appointments with people," Mrs. Lawson says shaking her head. "Rochelle just doesn't know herself, she just doesn't know who she is or where she's going. I think she's bouncing around like a rubber ball, running from one extreme to another looking for something that she can relate to. Have you seen the latest group she's been running around with? They seem nice and friendly and all, but they're sort of weird. I mean, I'm not sure how straight this bunch of guys is, you know. I think some of 'em are probably gay or something. And I just can't figure out what she wants to hang out with gay men for. Why can't she find a nice normal man to go out with? I mean she is quite attractive. I just don't understand why she's so confused and why she seems to be refusing the help of a nice young man like you."

She sighs. "I don't know, somehow things just seemed different when I was a kid. People seemed to care for each other more in those days. But times are different today. I see so many girls about Rochelle's age pushing their little babies around in strollers. I tell you, it's like babies having babies. These kids today need more help, more support, more attention than they're getting. You know what I'm talking about. The problem is at home, in the family, primarily. What with both parents working, or like me, the only parent in the house working full time, there's just less of a chance for the parent to be around for the child. Here I am, forty-one years old, mother of five children, grandmother of four children, working at nights so I can put myself through school in the day. What kind of time do you think I have to look after things? And I don't have any family around to help out. These teenage mothers need help raising their little babies, but all the grandparents, aunts and uncles and cousins are all off working or living too far away to be of any help. Yes, even grandparents like me are scraping to make a living. So how are we supposed to be there for our children and grandchildren?

"I tell you that's a good reason why I'm glad Our Place is there. They're doin' what the family used to do but just doesn't seem able to do anymore. Families don't seem to have the time to take care of children the way they should, and I think that's certainly true with our teenagers. And from what I know, the kids are going to Our Place 'cause you all are caring for them and listening to them and talking to them the way they need to be. Now, nothing as far as I can see is gonna take the place of the family. But, you know, like the church, Our Place is a place that can help families with their children, 'specially if their girls are pregnant or already have had a child. And like I was saying, given how things are in many families these days, it's a good thing that place and those people are over there looking after our kids during the day. Otherwise, who knows what some of these kids would be into."

She notices a smudge on the table and wipes it off with a towel. "I don't know," she says in an exhausted tone, "someone's dealt these kids a raw deal. I mean, do you think the young people of today have any real moral values?

"During the sixties all our kids heard was 'Black is Beautiful,' but no one took the time to show them *how* to be beautiful. Ask any woman. Sometimes you've got to work at being beautiful. These kids just thought that if you were black you were bad and you didn't have to do anything else. Just sit around and be angry and bad. Yes, the idea that it was tellin' kids to be proud of who you are is a blessing, don't get me wrong on that. That's one thing this generation might, and I said might, mind you, have over my generation. What I'm trying to say is that somewhere along the line some of these kids didn't get the message that part of being beautiful is to be educated and hardworking. Some of these kids have this live-for-the moment mentality. They've got enough trouble planning for the weekend, let alone when and how and with whom to have a baby. I don't know."

She has stopped talking for what seems to be a long moment. She smiles and stares ahead at the window, catching a reflection of herself in its glass.

"Maybe I don't have some of those problems because of where I came from.

"You know, I didn't always look the way I do now. When I was Rochelle's age I was even lighter skinned than I am now, and a lot thinner. Let me show you." Mrs. Lawson walks toward me and hands me a large red photo album and opens it. "You can see," she says, pointing to a photograph, "how white I look there. My sister, though, was darker than me. Here, look at this one of me when I was a baby. I look real white there. We've got a lot of mixed blood in my family: white, black, and even some Indian. My father was white and his mother was white, but his father was part Indian, a Blackfoot, I think. Now my mother," she says, as she turns the page and points to another photograph, "was mixed, too. Her mother was white and her father was black. My mother died when I was seven. She was a young woman when she died. My father raised me and my sister, mostly. And since my father was white and I was pretty white, he tried to raise me as if I was white. I remember this one boarding school he once sent me to. He really wanted me to become as white as possible so that I could fit into white society and marry a white man. He even had me believing that when I first went to this school. But I just couldn't fool them. I just didn't look white enough, despite my father's wishes. And when they found out that my mother was half black, that did it. Let me tell you, I didn't stay at that school very long.

"There were times when I was a little girl we'd go

visit my great aunt on my mother's side, the Schmidts," she explains, showing me a picture. "She raised my mother after my mother's parents died. Anyways, I remember there was all this German stuff in their house—a flag, a picture of Hitler, and even some Nazi uniforms!"

"Are you kidding!" I blurt out.

"My great aunt and her husband were real racists. Still they ended up raising my mother, who was half black.

"You see, my mother's mother and father killed themselves right after my mother was born. Sort of Romeo and Juliet style. According to my great aunt, my grandfather was a black sailor and my grandmother was a nice white girl who went wrong. I guess they figured that they wouldn't be allowed to be together in this world, so they were going to be together in the next. They really must have loved each other. Anyways, my great aunt raised my mother as her own."

She turns the page to show me a picture of her father's mother. "As I think about it now, there's a lot more to my family's racial history than I have really thought about in quite a long time. When my father married my mother, his father disowned him because he married a black woman. That really must have been a scandal. Anyways, when I was nineteen, I married William Lawson, my sweetheart from high school. And when I told my father that I was going to marry William, he told me he would disown me if I did." She rubs her fingers nervously along the edge of the photograph. "William was the blackest boy I knew and I wanted him. I guess I was really rebelling against my parents, like a lot of teenagers do. And since my mother was dead, I rebelled against my father. The rest is history. I married William, had five children by him, and later divorced him.

"Who knows, maybe I was havin' what they call an 'identity crisis' or something like that. With all the racial stuff and mixture in my family, how the hell was I supposed to know who I was. I guess I was just trying to find out. It's funny when you think about it; I did just what my grandmother did, and my father did to me just what his father did to him. See, he died of a heart attack three days after I was married."

I look at the photograph of her father that sits in my lap.

"What's a parent today, anyways?" she asks quietly. "Nothing. A parent today is nothing but somebody to foot the bills."

Mrs. Lawson stands up and walks toward the door. I follow her. She rests a hand on the doorknob.

"I guess that's what really gets me. The older I get the less I understand. In a world filled with famine and starvation and poverty and atomic warfare, nobody seems to care, nobody seems to have any compassion anymore. 'So what' is all I hear people saying these days, 'it doesn't affect me.' That kind of thinking makes me so mad. Where are people's values these days, anyways? Hell, maybe these young people think that the world is gonna be blown up by some atomic bomb so they figure it's best to, what's the phrase, 'live for today 'cause I might die tomorrow.' They're sure doing that, I tell you. Hell, maybe they're right, maybe we're all gonna go up in one big bang that we might not even hear.

"Maybe they're the smart ones and I'm the dumb

one, spending all my time and money supporting a family and going back to school to be a social worker, no less. What for? If the bomb comes there won't be nothin' I can do, even as a lousy social worker. Maybe I ought to go out and have some fun like the kids do. They're *always* looking for pleasure; rush, rush, rush, like they're bouncing all over the place. Ain't there any laws or rules anymore? It seems like there's no one in control. Who *is* in control around here, anyway? The kids? The parents? You've got me. What they need is some good old-fashioned patience. I just hope these young people, like my Rochelle, don't hurt themselves along the way. If you're always rushing through life, bouncing from one extreme to the other you're bound to end up losing stuff, including yourself.

"Anyway, I'll tell Rochelle you came by looking for her." She opens the screen door, I walk onto the front porch. We wave to each other. Mrs. Lawson calls out as I walk down the driveway. "Rochelle needs someone like you to talk to. More of these kids could use it, too. And I'll tell you something else, there are times when us adults need someone to talk to, you know?" She laughs. "You ought to come around here and talk to me sometimes, too!"

What an afternoon, I think as I walk back to the center. What an incredible afternoon. I wonder if Rochelle knows half of what her mother has told me.

IV

I ride a long and large hospital elevator. I wander the winding corridors in search of room 8220. Rochelle had been rushed to the emergency room two days before for an operation on her ruptured appendix. It has been over a month since I talked with her mother. It has been nearly three months since I have talked to Rochelle.

A distant voice answers my knock on the door. Rochelle is perched up in her bed, staring almost aimlessly at the television that looms from across the room.

"I'm just catchin' the last few minutes of one of the soap operas I like. It's gettin' real good," she explains as she smiles.

"You know what my mother says about the soaps? She says people watch 'em in order to feel reassured about themselves; you know, that their lives aren't as miserable as the people in the soaps. She says people will tell you they watch 'em 'cause they think it's 'interesting,' or 'cause they get some kind of vicarious thrill out of it, or 'cause they're bored or something. But my mother says, don't let them fool you. Way deep down inside they're on pins and needles comparin' their lives to the lives of those folks on TV, hopin' to God that they're better off. The real 'thrill,' I think, is that they're probably overjoyed at knowin' that, though they might have it bad, it could sure be a lot worse!

"These soaps ain't that bad, really. I think they can make you feel some sympathy for someone else. I mean, look at this show will ya," she says, pointing up to the television set. "All these rich white folks got plenty of money and stuff, but they got lots of problems, too. It makes me feel that although I ain't got much, I don't got it as bad as they do. At least these days I don't. So, I feel real sorry for them."

We talk for a while about her operation and how she is feeling.

"The room here is pretty nice, don't you think, Dan?" she remarks noticing that I am looking around the room.

"And those flowers, ain't they lovely? A friend brought them. He was real nice to do that. I'll tell you one thing, being in the hospital sure tells you who your friends are. It's been all right bein' here this time; I've had lots of people come by to see me. My mother's been up here every day. So's my sister and my little nephew. You know, you're the first person from Our Place I've seen in a long time. I've been so busy lately, I haven't had the time to come by. Say, Dan, how's the writing comin'?"

"I think it's going well," I answer, surprised that she has thought to ask. "In fact, I think I'll be ready very soon to try a first draft that I can show you. How's that sound to you?"

"I guess that sounds fine," Rochelle replies flatly. For a long moment we are both quiet. I watch her gently massage that part of her left arm where the nurse has fastened her IV. As she rubs her arm, her eyes seem to withdraw, to pull away from our conversation, from my presence, from our shared presence in that room. She starts to cry. Although she cries softly, she continues to cry for several minutes, a low, moanful weep.

I wonder about my presence in her room.

She continues to cry.

I reach out and touch her.

"I'm okay, Dan, really. Sorry, I don't know what it is. This damn IV is killing me," she whispers in a faint voice. For a moment she is quiet again. "You know, I've been in the hospital so many times, and for things a lot worse than having my appendix taken out. And compared with what some other people are in here for, I know I'm pretty lucky. But you'd think that my father might come see me. Damn, listen to me talk silly. Why should I still expect him to pay attention to me? He never did before."

She shakes her head.

"I used to have to tell him straight to his face, 'You have no right to whup me if you don't do anything for me.' And then he'd look at me and say, 'Girl, who are you to talk like that?' But he knew it was the truth. He'd whup me. But I wouldn't care.

"He called me earlier today. He said, 'Is there anything you need?' I said, 'No, I just need your Blue Cross number.' Serious. 'Cause if I didn't have that insurance I don't know how I'd pay for this. I'd have to claim for bankruptcy at the age of eighteen. That's no joke either. I woulda been owin' this hospital a lot of money for my second baby if I hadn'ta had insurance. His bill was over ten thousand dollars 'cause he was in the preemie unit. I guess it just cost a lot of money to have them preemie babies all wired up. Ten thousand dollars. I would have been paying that for the rest of my life. And that was cheap, too."

"Cheap?" I ask with surprise.

"Yeah, my friend Cheryl was in the hospital with me at the same time and her bill was over twenty-five thousand dollars. But she was on welfare, so they paid for it. Her baby was in there for over two months while mine was only there eight days before he died."

Rochelle leans her head back deep into the pillow and stares quietly at the ceiling. She sighs slowly, turning her eyes toward the window and then over to the vase of flowers that sits on the window sill.

She turns her head toward me.

"Did I ever tell you that my baby, Alan Lee, died in my arms? That's one night I'll never forget.

"He lived only eight days. You see, I had him when I was in my seventh month. I was supposed to have an operation to put a clamp on my cervix 'cause I was dilatin' too fast, you know, I was openin' up too wide too early. The doctors had told me that my water bag might break during the operation, but I had to have the operation or I might have my baby too soon. Well, the morning I was supposed to have the operation, sure enough, my bag broke and they rushed me to the hospital. My friend, Cheryl, was already in the hospital and she was a real big help to me during the birth. And my baby's father, Michael, he was up there too. They was singin' and playin' around tryin' to keep my mind off the pain and stuff. He was dressed up in this ol' surgical gown, crackin' jokes. It was real crazy. And when the baby was born, Michael was all up in the mirrors and stuff, tryin' to see the baby come out. He was so happy it was a boy.

"Yeah, but then right after my son was born, Michael took off and went with Alan Lee and the nurses and everybody, passin' out cigars and shit, leaving me all alone by myself in that room. I'll never forget that feelin'. I mean, it was good and all that Michael was there, but then leavin' me like that, that didn't help me at all. And then he started actin' all stupid about naming the baby. He wanted to name the baby some stupid ol' name, I can't even remember what it was. My baby didn't have a name for about three days 'cause we was all arguin' about what to name him. Then my mother said, 'How about Alan Lee? That's a pretty name.' So she's the one who named him.

"Havin' him wasn't that hard, actually. They induced my labor. They put somethin' in my IV to make me start contractin'. My mother was there the whole time and she said I did real good. I had a natural childbirth. I didn't get no pain killers, no nothin'. And after I had my baby I couldn't believe it," she explains with a renewed excitement. "It was like, oooo, *I* had a baby! You know, 'cause it was somethin' livin' you know, and they put him on me and stuff. He was real, real pretty. It really freaked me out, that I gave birth to that little boy. I was so excited. I think I stayed in the preemie unit more than I stayed in my bed.

"You know what's funny?" she remarks, after pausing. "I never thought for a second that he wouldn't live. I wasn't even thinking' about him dyin'. I just knew he was gonna live. I was still runnin' around buyin' him stuff. That baby had everything. Shit, mostly everything my little nephew's got was my baby's. His bed, some t-shirts. My mother even bought him a little outfit. He had everything. But he just didn't make it."

Rochelle reaches for a glass of water that sits on the bedstand to her left. She drinks several swallows, taking a short breath of air between each.

"The first night I had my baby I was up in that preemie room all night, rubbin' on his nose and all kinds of stuff. The nurse up there said, 'Don't you ever go to bed?' I said, 'No.' She said, 'Your stitches don't hurt?' I said, 'No.'

"It was pretty great up there. They've got a real good preemie unit here, with a real nice parent room where you can spend the night. So, even though he was all hooked up to this respirator with all kinds of wires and tubes and stuff, I'd visit him all the time. I wanted him to know that his mother was there. That's real important for kids, you know. Anyways, I'd like to touch him on his nose. It was my special way of lettin' him know I was there. I even told them nurses not to touch him on his nose, that that was my signal to him that his mother was there by his side.

"I just knew my baby was gonna live; he was bigger than this other preemie baby in the ward. I was just so sure. Then on about the fourth day I had this sense, this premonition that something was wrong, so I decided to stay up in the hospital for the night. I remember the nurse asking me again, 'Don't you ever go home?' I told her, 'I'm here 'cause I love my baby!' You know, them nurses was nice and all, but I just can't help feelin' that everybody there was all up in my business, knowin' everything about me. It's like they was investigatin' me or somethin.' "

"Like me?" I ask, feeling a bit guilty.

"No, not really. You see with them, them knowin' about me is sort of out of my control. It seems like the only time people get interested in me and ask me how I'm feelin' and stuff is when I'm in trouble or in a hospital. With you, it's sort of different. It's 'cause I want to tell you stuff. It's my choice.

"Anyway, that night I saw how his little arms and legs were lookin' sort of swollen and then I noticed that even his little head was swollen with water. When I saw that I started panickin'. I just couldn't believe that there was somethin' the matter. The nurse told me that my baby was havin' serious problems with his kidneys and he couldn't pass any water. He was gettin' all bloated 'cause his water couldn't go nowhere. Then she told me that he might die. Well, I started freakin' right then and there. I just couldn't believe what this nurse was tellin' me was the truth. I was just so scared, Dan. I took the bus home that night and I was crying so hard and all these people were staring at me. They was lookin' at me like I was crazy. One man tried to talk to me and I just turned around and spit on him. I was so upset, no one could say nothin' to me.

"I went straight over to the church and asked this Father there to pray with me, for my baby was dying. This man was so wonderful to me. He's the sole reason I'm still alive today. If it weren't for this man, I'da killed myself for sure. At first I felt I had no reason to keep on livin'. I had no one to talk to, no friends, no loving family, no one. Then I met Father. He got down on his knees and prayed with me. He cried with me for nearly an hour. Then he put his hands on my shoulder and I felt this immediate sense of release, you know, a feeling of ease and peace. It was as if all my burdens and problems was just lifted up off of my shoulders and out of my soul. It was an incredible experience. I'll never forget it, or that man's true kindness. After that he would come up to the hospital with me. He'd make me eat. He'd say, 'How can your baby be strong if you're not strong?' He also baptized my baby.

"On the day my baby died the nurse showed me on this screen how his heartbeat was slowin' down. There I was, watchin' my baby die, heartbeat by heartbeat. So I told her to take him off the respirator and let me hold him until he dies. And that was like fifteen minutes until he died. But I held him for about two hours. I felt him get cold. The nurse brought him to me all wrapped up in a blanket. I unwrapped him, though, and held him close to my skin to let his cold little body feel my warmth. I took him into the parent's room and cried to him, 'I'm sorry you had to die, I really wanted you to live. You'll be all right.' I was cryin' out his name and stuff. He was real pretty.

"And while I was crying, I was thinking, you know, plotting to take him out of the hospital with me that very night. I was gonna take him home with me as if he were alive. Could you imagine that? Me walking past all them nurses and doctors with my baby all wrapped up, pretending it was alive and foolin' everybody!" she conjectures with a smile. "I'd have taken him home. Simple. I hadn't thought the rest of it out, but I just wanted him home with me so badly, you know, so that he could see his room and crib and all his clothes and stuff.

"I just knew he knew I was his mother. I wanted to make sure that he knew I was there, you know, 'cause so many girls have their babies in the preemie unit and their babies never get to really see their parents. And to me, it's important, 'cause babies can sense their mother being there, or someone carin' for 'em. And that was important to me.

"I'm kind of glad, I mean, I'm not glad that he died, but I'm better off now without a child, I see. God just didn't want me to have it then. 'Cause right after my baby died, I got a job at a day-care center. That was like weird, you know, working with kids. But it was great. It showed me that I really didn't need a kid, that it was a lot of hassle—not a hassle, you know, but you had to go through a lot. You had to give up a lot, time and money, which I didn't have at the time. And now that I know that, next time I get pregnant, I'll probably be married. I know I'll have a career and I'll be financially secure with my own house and everything. Otherwise, I won't bring a child into this world. Not me, not havin' anythin'. What do I have to offer that child? I have love, but that isn't enough. A child needs clothes on his back, food in his mouth, shelter. And I don't want to be going from place to place or bein' on no welfare. 'Cause they'll cut that out on you in a minute. And they'll be all up in your business: 'Who'd you do it with? Who's the daddy? Why ain't he here?' No way I want to go through all that.

"You know, a lot of girls have their babies to try and keep their boyfriends. After Michael told me he wasn't gonna help support our baby, I told him to go away and don't never come back in our lives. I didn't care. My bein' pregnant was no accident. I knew all about birth control and stuff. It's just simple, Dan. I wanted to get pregnant, and Michael just happened to be the father."

"Why was that so important to you?" I ask.

"You really want to know? I wanted that baby so bad, 'cause I had lost my other baby, my first one. He died of a miscarriage when I was fifteen. I wanted something I could put my love into, something that could love me."

Her voice cracks and her eyes begin to water. She speaks slowly.

"I didn't know how else to do that. I felt I had no sisters that I could sit down and talk to, my mother was going through a lot of stuff herself, so I didn't have anybody. And, to me, I feel if I'm to survive, I got to survive for someone else. If I'm to live here on this earth, I feel like I have to live for someone, sort of, taking care of someone and stuff like that. I always have to be doing something like that or else I'd feel the world wasn't worth livin' in. 'Cause ain't nothin' in this world I really, really want, you know; material things aren't really anything. I'm not gonna trash 'em, but what are diamonds and rubies and all that? You can't lie in bed and say, 'I love you, ruby, I love you, diamond.' Money never really meant that much to me. Oh, I had nice clothes 'cause my appearance meant a lot to me. Most of the time, though, I did have money 'cause I worked. But my mother never would buy me anything. She'd always buy my sister everything," she whispers, "so I'd be jealous, too. She got everything." She sobs softly.

"And like I said, Dan, if it weren't for Father, I'd probably be dead now. After my miscarriage I tried to kill myself three times. The last time I tried was the day before me and the father of my first baby were gonna get our blood test for a marriage license. We were both sixteen then. I was in Indiana at his father's house at the time. I felt all alone, I didn't even *want* to get married. I didn't know what I was doing. I just wanted to die so bad. I took a whole bunch of these pink and white pills I found up in the medicine chest. Pretty soon I was hallucinatin'; man, it was a real trip; it was real crazy," she says, as she now laughs.

"After I'd been walkin' around for a while I went into his father's car which was in the garage and started yellin' out his name, 'Tony, Tony!' I was hoping he could hear me 'cause I could see him shovelin' snow right outside the garage. It was December, as I remember. Anyways, he didn't know who was callin' him; he was lookin' all around, it was real funny. Well it wasn't long after that that those little pink and white capsules had entered my whole system and the next thing I knew I was in the hospital surrounded by all these crazy people. Did you know that they send OD people to the crazy ward in the hospital? I guess you've got to be a little out of your mind to try and OD in the first place, but Dan, I was no crazy, I just needed someone to talk to. I guess I wish Our Place was around then.

"I tell you, all these years I feel like I've been too nice to people. It just seems like I end up carin' more for them than they do for me. Like take my eighth grade graduation, for example. It's no small thing graduating from eighth grade. It's a real important time in your life. And my mother just got me some ol' dress. I mean it was nice and everything, but she didn't get it for me with all the, you know, ceremony and fuss that's supposed to go with it. She didn't take me with her like other mothers did for their daughters. And no one in my family even came to my graduation, can you believe that? Not one person. I felt terrible, real angry, if you know what I mean.

"Shit, I've wanted a regular mother-daughter relationship for years, but I gave up on that a long time ago. Now don't get me wrong, Dan, I love my mother. She's had a tough life raisin' five kids by herself, working full time and now trying to go to college on top of that. And didn't really have no mother to show her how to be a mother. Well, I'm actually proud of my mother. And I hate all these people who try and tell me I'm black and make me feel bad 'cause my mother's white. I'm black and I'm white and I'm even part Indian. We're all mixed up. Differences is not what it's all about. It's about caring for one another. Period. I don't care if you're orange and purple. What matters is life. Maybe that's why if I got pregnant again I feel I wouldn't have an abortion. Except, that is, if I ever got raped."

Her adamant tone is not betrayed by the slow sigh she has exhaled. I realize I have sighed also.

"Rochelle, can I ask you a question I've been thinking about for a while?"

"Sure."

"What happened all those times you didn't show up for our meetings?"

She clears her throat.

"To tell you the truth, I'm not really sure. When I'd see you and agree to meet you at a certain time, I really intended on going, but when the time actually came, I wouldn't. I think some of it was I was reacting against something my mother said. You see, I used to like comin' by Our Place to talk with you and study and stuff. It was a real important time for me. But then my mother once said to me, 'Oh, isn't Dan Frank a nice young man? You should talk with him more.' I guess I felt whatever she was pushin', I didn't want any part of 'cause then it wouldn't really be my choice, it wouldn't really be special. I sort of like talkin' to you like I liked talking to Father."

Reaching in front of her, Rochelle smooths out her blankets and pulls them up snugly around her chest.

"You know what I'd like to do if I had a lot of money? I'd start a center like Our Place, but a bigger one, one that's like totally equipped with everything a kid or teenager would need. Schooling, job training, parenting help for teen parents. It would be a big, warm place with lots of happy colors and good food. If you wanted you could even sleep there. And as I think of it in my mind, this would be a place for kids who had run away from home, or who wanted to, or for kids who have nowhere to go, or no one wanted them or cared for them. It would be a place where people had people to talk to."

Suddenly, she changes the subject. Yet, she continues to speak as if she were simply continuing her thought.

"And you know, Father did another important thing for me. After my baby died, I had him cremated and I wanted to keep his urn. But Father said not to 'cause it was like tryin' to hold on to my baby, and you can't do that. By sayin' that, I think Father helped me accept the fact that Alan Lee was gone. It was a pretty urn, all different colors of blue. He's buried out with my mother's parents, so I know he's being looked after."

Her sudden change of subject jars my concentration. I look at her resting on her back staring at the white serene ceiling. She has stopped speaking. I am quiet, too.

I remember: One afternoon Rochelle said goodbye to me after I had driven her home from Our Place. She had stepped out of the car and begun to close the door. Pausing briefly, she then opened it slightly and said, "Hey, you've got to lock these doors. You know how people are these days, you've got to be safe. You might get jumped at the stoplight or something." She then locked the door.

I remember: Rochelle has just asked me about my writing. But she must have been thinking about her father because it was about him that she began to speak. My presence in that room and her presence in that hospital must have triggered for Rochelle memories and feelings of events experienced but forgotten long ago. Perhaps she feels that like her father, I, too, will soon be gone, now that I have my "material."

I remember: She has been describing her vision of an ideal place for young people and their children and

then abruptly changed the subject to her baby's crema-
tion. "He's buried out with my mother's parents, so I
know he's being looked after." Was that her way of
asking, "Who's going to look after me?"

I remember the photographs Mrs. Lawson had
shown me: Rochelle's great-grandparents, the black
sailor and the white girl; Mrs. Lawson and her husband, William, and his black, black face; Mrs. Lawson's father and his father, the great disowner.

And I remember stories I had been told: About the
moment at that white boarding school when Frances
Lawson's cover was blown; about the night Rochelle
ran down the street, running swiftly and furiously from
her father and his belt; about the chilling December air
as Rochelle sat in that car in the Indiana garage halluci-
nating and dying simultaneously; about how Rochelle
felt as Alan Lee's body lost its warmth.

And I remember: Seeing the title of Rochelle's book,
Nobody Is Listening to Me.

And in her hospital room, somewhere in the pause
between her words, I remember one more voice. It is
the voice of a preacher, heard on my car radio one
afternoon, so many months ago, as I drove to meet
Rochelle.

The preacher warned: "We've got to stop screaming
at our young people, 'These are the rules around here.'
We've got to listen to them, we've got to talk to them,
we've got to study with them, we've got to know that
underneath that sometimes rough exterior is a fragile
person, looking for simple acceptance."

I remember: On that afternoon when I was listening
to the preacher on my car radio, so many months ago,
Rochelle had already decided not to meet me as we had
planned.

Plans

Carmela Watson is seventeen and ambitious.

She works full time at Washington National Insurance Company, winning two promotions in one year.

She's going for her third.

She saves her money.

To graduate from high school, Carmela lacks only her gym credits. But she hasn't time for that. Instead, she comes to prepare for her GED exam every Wednesday promptly at five-thirty. She comes dressed up; make-up modestly adorns her face.

Carmela has a son, Eric, Jr., three months old. She has a boyfriend, Eric, the baby's father. They have plans together. He, too, works at Washington National. Eric is eighteen.

Carmela feels she is different from some of the other girls.

"Me and Eric had been looking for an apartment to rent together. We looked for a while, too. We were going to live together. But my mother didn't like that idea too well. She believes in marriage. So do I. Eric and I'll get married. But not now. Maybe after we each finish college. We both agree we're too young to be married. We both feel we need time to grow some before we're ready for that. We're not adults yet, you know.

"I tell you, Dan, it ain't no big thing to have a baby and not be married. We have each other and we're planning on it always bein' that way."

She shrugs her shoulders.

"Now, I don't plan on bein' at Washington National forever. Eventually, I'd like to either be a nurse or a child psychologist. But I don't want to be in school for ten or twelve years! I make good money at my job. So does Eric. One reason we're not going to live together now is so we can save our rent money so we can buy a place in a couple of years. That was my mother's idea. Besides, Eric only lives around the corner from me. He's real involved with our son. Get this, he gets angry at me if he can't have the baby over at his house at least four times a week! His mother's real good with the baby, too. We got it such that Eric's godmother sits for little Eric while we're at work for only thirty dollars a week. That's half price! Eric's cousin works at a department store, so we get big boxes of paper diapers for only two dollars each! So we're able to save something. Money's no real problem. My parents are divorced. My father sends me money. My grandmother gives me money, too."

With the flat of her hand, she pats the top of her math book.

"This GED is my ticket out of this place. My mother, she'll sit with the baby anytime she sees me pull my books out. Eventually, I'd like to move out of this town. Certainly by the time he's ready for school. I'd like to move to the deep south. My family's from there.

It's beautiful country. Safer than up here. Don't need locks on your door."

I ask, "With all these plans, did you plan on having little Eric?"

"Heck no! Are you kidding! Accident. Pure accident. I used birth control but it must not have worked. I use a different method now. I didn't believe in abortions. Eric didn't either. He said to do whatever I want to. But he really wanted me to have the baby. If my baby's father was some guy I was runnin' with for just a month or so, I might have had the abortion anyways, even though I don't believe in them. But I knew Eric. I'd been goin' with him for three years."

She looks at me as she adjusts the lace collar on her white cotton blouse. "I'm out working. I got goals. And one goal is not to have me no more babies for a long time to come. You don't see me coming up here like these other girls, do you? They like to talk junk and fight. Black girls like to do that. Some of 'em have their babies and is back up here havin' more. They're just stupid. Don't even take care of the ones they've got. Their mothers or grandmothers or aunts do. But not me."

Carmela taps her pencil on the table.

"This baby wasn't in my plans at all. But I'm makin' it. Me and Eric together. Got to. I got plans."

In Between

I

Casual talk in a casual place.

Like so many I've had at Our Place.

Like no other I've had at Our Place.

We stand in the hall, near the table just outside the library. Valerie Wallace is five months pregnant.

She speaks first. "I've gotta take the U.S. Constitution test and the one for the State of Illinois, too."

I say, "You must know Monica Downing and Rulla Martin. They're studying for the Constitution test, too."

"Huh?" she says as she chews her gum.

"You know," I insist, "Monica Downing and Rulla Martin?"

She furrows her brow and turns the corner of her upper lip.

"They're in your class at school. In eleventh grade."

"Eleventh grade? What are you talkin' about? I need help with the Constitution test all right, but not no eleventh-grade test. Shoot, mister, I'm talkin' about the eighth-grade Constitution test. I'm still only in eighth grade."

II

A half a year later my thirteen-year-old friend and I talk over lunch at her favorite fast-food restaurant. She eats a double cheeseburger, fries, and a pop. We've come here twice before.

This time there are three of us. Valerie's two-month-old son Conrad sits quietly in his portable baby-chair, sucking his bottle of milk.

"Now that I have Conrad, he's the most important thing to me. Then comes my grandmother, myself, my sister, my mother, my cousin, my boyfriend, my father, and my stepfather. Before he was born, my grandmother was the most important to me. See, she raised me. When I was four, my mother moved North, but I didn't want to go. I liked it where we was in Mississippi. So I stayed with my grandmother. Oh, I'd see my mother 'bout once or twice a year. Every year I'd come to Evanston to see her and my cousins. That's where I met my boyfriend."

She smiles.

"I remember when I was ten, my mother gave me a baby doll for Christmas. That's what I really wanted more than anything was a baby doll. One of my very own. I said, 'What a swell sister!' Everyone was shocked. They all laughed. My mother said, 'I ain't your sister, fool! I'm your mother!' "

Through a straw, she sips her pop.

"I still like to play and run around, but when I was pregnant I couldn't go roller skatin', though. And before Conrad was born I still liked to play with my baby dolls. I'd still like to, but he's enough for right now. I even still like to play on the floor and play with my toes. Doe-dee-doe!" she sings and then blushes.

She dips a french fry in a pool of ketchup.

"I came to Evanston 'cause my grandmother was sick and I was thrown out of school too many times for fightin' with the boys. They was all callin' me 'fast.' And the girls, too. So I told them off. But girls can be real jealous, let me tell you. My girlfriend told me, 'You ain't the only one who's gonna get pregnant.' I told her, 'It's only fun while you're pregnant, not afterwards. So I wouldn't if I were you.' But she'll prob'ly wind up pregnant anyways 'cause she's always wantin' to be out in front of me. She thinks I've got somethin' special up on her. But I don't really, y'know. I just got me a baby. See, I didn't intend on gettin' pregnant. I was messin' around after school at my friend's house. There were two other couples, too. We'd go there 'cause there was no parents around. But my girlfriend she seems like she's intendin' to get herself pregnant.

"When I got pregnant I was real scared about my boyfriend and my mother's reaction. But when I told my mother she just laughed, 'My first grandchild!' She was real happy, so it made me feel like I could be happy about it, too. I'd been feelin' sorta funny about havin' a baby, you know? My mother had me when she was sixteen, I think. But I'd been interested in boys since I was at least ten. That's when I had my first boyfriend. We'd send notes to each other in class: 'Do you love me?' Then we'd have to check a little box that said, 'yes' or 'no.' "

Valerie now holds Conrad in her arms.

"Bein' pregnant made me feel like crying a lot of the time. Sometimes I'd just start cryin' for no real reason. My sister and my cousins would call me a cry baby. I'd come to Our Place 'cause I was feelin' lonely. At home they all just like watching TV and I don't. At least at Our Place I got people to be with and talk to, even if it's just, you know, talk."

She wipes Conrad's lips.

"You know, sometimes I look at him and he don't seem like he's mine. I guess I'm not used to him yet. Even in the hospital, right after he was born he didn't seem like he was mine. It's hard to think he's what I had in me for nine months. After he came out of me, the doctor put him on my stomach. 'Get that messy thing off me!' I yelled at that doctor. Maybe he don't seem like he's mine 'cause he can't talk yet. Now, my little cousin, he's different. He's three years old and he seems like he's mine, but he ain't. He's my auntie's. But I just about raised him myself. He talks. That's how I know he's attached to me."

Still holding her son, she looks at him as she talks.

"It's funny, I know he ain't a baby doll, but he don't yet seem like he's a real baby, like my cousin. He's sorta in between."

Memory

Barbara Kenney rests her head on the edge of the table at which we work. She has dropped her pencil in the crease of her math book. She cannot solve a word problem. The problem is nearly identical to the previous three problems she has answered correctly. We have worked on this set of problems for two weeks. She has lost her concentration. She loses it often. Her memory goes blank. She remembers nothing.

Yet, every Wednesday, for three months, Barbara has come to Our Place for tutoring. A friend of hers had told her that I could help her prepare to take the GED exam.

Barbara is eighteen. Her classmates at Evanston Township High School will graduate in a month. Barbara left high school because she did not have enough credits to graduate. Barbara has a son. Reggie is fourteen months old.

We have been studying for forty-five minutes.

"You mad at me?" Barbara asks, still resting her head on the table.

She has sensed my frustration.

"You're mad at me, I can tell. I'm sure mad at me. I just can't do these dumb problems.

"I always forget how you do 'em. You give me home-work to do, problems just like the ones we'd been workin' on. Then when I try to do 'em on my own, I forget. Just can't concentrate."

Barbara raises her head. She speaks softly. "You know I'm tryin' to make somethin' of myself. I really want my GED. My mother says I can't do it. She says it's selfish, too. She says I should be with my baby or out lookin' for a job. She just don't realize I'm doin' this for both of us, for me and Reggie. I'm tryin' to better myself, but she don't believe I can do it."

In our three months of working together this shy girl hasn't talked about much except her math work. When she waits for her lesson, Barbara sits quietly in a chair in the hall. She knows some of the other girls from the neighborhood. She smiles if someone says hello. But, generally, she keeps to herself.

"I started out bad in ninth grade. I was better before then, you know, in grade school and junior high. I mean, I didn't catch on to everything the teacher was talkin' about, but nobody does, right? See, I started ninth grade late. In December. I had some trouble in the summer. Just before graduation from eighth."

Barbara picks up her pencil. She doodles on the margin of a page in her math book. Without talking, she looks at me for a long moment.

"See, I was raped. I couldn't go to school like the other kids at the beginning of school. I started late 'n it messed everything up. It was just before graduatin' that I was raped. Me and my girl friend was walkin' back one night from a party. I guess it was pretty late. These three men started followin' us down the street. I recog-nized one of 'em. He'd been at the party. They had a car, too. One man says, 'You want to get in the car or should we help you?' He was wavin' a gun at us as he said it. They blindfolded us and we drove off. I don't even know how long we was there. My girl friend says at least a whole day. I don't really remember. They took us to some apartment in Chicago. They all took their turn. I think I closed my eyes. They hurt me more 'n my girl friend 'cause I tried to fight back. I know they intended to kill us. But one of the men tricked on the others and gave us some money for the El and helped us escape."

Barbara sighs.

"I only see my girl friend once in a while now. She's changed a lot since then. We'd talk a lot about it to each other. See, she's a prostitute now. And she gets angry at me when I tell her she should be tryin' to get herself together 'n get off the streets. I tell her how I'm tryin' to get myself back in school through my GED 'n she says, 'Who are you to tell me what to do!' It makes me feel bad when she says that to me. But I guess I can understand. We're just different people.

"She goes from boyfriend to boyfriend. From here to here to here," she says as she moves her hand across the table. "I guess that's how she's tryin' to get over it. Or maybe it just shows she can't get over it. She bounces all over, from one boy to another. She just can't be too close with no one, not even me.

"I'm different, though. I sort of get attached to one man. I don't like lettin' go. My other thing is I feel I rush into things too fast. You know what I'm tryin' to say?

"I really wanted to feel comfortable with men, see. But I feel I did it maybe too fast. See, I met my boyfriend, William, not even two years after, you know, I got raped. He really liked me. And he really listened to me as to how I felt about things, about bein' raped. It didn't bother him. I really wanted to feel normal around men. Y'know? William wanted me to have his baby 'n I wanted one, too. I felt if I had a baby, I'd be a normal woman, and normal people would like me like they did before.

"Me and William still see each other, when one of us isn't out firing the other. He fired me last week. We usually get together again soon, though. Still, I got high. I do that when I feel bad. Stayed high most of the week. I guess I don't study too well when I'm high, huh?

"I still feel funny around a gang of dudes. That's why I don't like walkin' around the street in front of the center by myself. I know they won't hurt me or nothin', but I don't like them callin' on me like they do. Bad memories, you know."

Her maze of pencil-drawn lines thickens.

"My girl friend remembers much more 'n I do about bein' raped. My memory of it isn't too good. She had to remind me of a lot since then. I used to remember things a lot better before then. Thing is , I can't forget; guess that's why I can't remember."

Tradition

I

Gwen White twists a small rubber doll at the waist. She wants this girl doll to sit on a miniature couch in the living room of the dollhouse that stands on the table before us. Like giants, my sixteen-year-old friend and I sit in the toddler-size chairs that circle the toddler-size table. A jack-in-the-box also sits on the table, it, too, left inadvertently by one of the young children. Around us, toys of many different kinds and shapes and colors lie along the walls and on the shelves.

Our Place has just reopened after a four-day Christmas holiday. By noon many teens have arrived and settled in the parents' room, where the staff has set up a portable black-and-white television for the girls to watch a special Christmas episode of a favorite soap opera. It is the child-care room where Gwen and I find a quiet place to talk.

"How was your Christmas?" I ask.
"Okay, I guess. But not too warm," she answers.
"It has been cold this week," I remark. "Last night the temperature dropped well below zero."
Gwen remains quiet. She leans forward in her chair. Her elbows rest on the table's edge. She continues to

bend the doll. Her silence tells me I have missed her message. She hadn't been talking about the weather at all.

"Christmas hasn't been warm since my grandmother's house burned down on New Year's Eve of the bicentennial winter. I was twelve then. I lived in that house since I was born. It was a big house. When it got burned, there was at least fifteen people living there. Other times, there'd be more."

She raises her head and looks at the ceiling.

"Let's see, two of my cousins slept on them roll-away cots near the china cabinet in the dining room. My brother and another cousin slept on the couches in the living room. Me, I slept upstairs in a room with my three sisters. We had us two double beds. My aunt slept with her little son in another room with a double bed. My uncle, my grandmother's brother, had himself his own room, like my grandmother did. Two more of my aunt's kids lived in the basement. Before they lived down there, they all slept up in my aunt's bed. And then there was the people my grandmother'd rent rooms to. We call 'em wineheads. There were three or four of them basement rooms.

"That house was always filled with people, Lord, it was crowded! And just when someone would move out and you'd think you got a little more room, my grandmother out of the goodness of her heart would take someone else in, for a night, for a month, or more. I had some other cousins who lived with us for a while. They were from St. Louis. Their mother couldn't take care of them or somethin'. I was too young at the time to know why they came to live with us."

Gwen crosses her legs. She places the doll on the couch.

"The fire started 'bout quarter to ten, just a couple of hours before New Year's. My cousins and my brother was lighting off fireworks at the time and watching whatshisname that do American Bandstand . . . Dick Clark on TV. I was in the living room with my cousin watching another show, 'One of My Wives Is Missing,' on channel seven. My cousin was pregnant and having her contractions real often and I was counting 'em for her. She'd be askin' 'What time is it?' all the time. That's how I knew what time the fire started. Everybody else was all upstairs. My grandmother was sleepin', and my cousins were all upstairs, too, prob'ly smokin' reefer 'n all, who knows. My mother was home visiting and was upstairs with my sister.

"I happened to be lookin' at the clock when all the lights went off, except for the kitchen light which had run of a different wire. So when I saw the lights go out I said, 'Dang!' 'cause the show was right at the rising part, right when they was gonna find his wife. Meanwhile, my cousin, she keeps callin' out 'What time is it? What time is it?' Then I saw the smoke right through the dining room floor! At first I thought it was smoke coming from the kitchen. My aunt was in there cookin'. She cooks real good chitlins when she's drunk with her big vodka bottle. But then I saw the smoke coming right up out of the linoleum floor! I started screaming, 'Fire! Fire! Fire!' No one believed me. I ran upstairs yellin'; I said, 'Mom!' I said, 'Charles!' I said, 'Denise! The house, it's on fire!' I got real pissed 'cause they didn't pay me no attention.

"A fire shot straight up over the banister to the top of the stairs. Then this other flame shoots up this hall window right where I was standing. The fire was burning inside the walls straight up to my uncle's bedroom window. There weren't no smoke up in the bedrooms yet, but where I was you could see it. The radiator all of a sudden started tingling. That kinda got me scared. I thought it was gonna blow up. My uncle came on 'arunnin' down with everyone else followin'!

"And all I could hear in my head was the guy from TV, Frazier Thomas, saying, 'When your house is on fire, don't stop for nothin'! Just get outta there!' I thought, 'Are you crazy?' I just bought me over a hundred dollars worth of clothes! I mean, it was Christmas time!"

She shakes her head and speaks slowly. "See, the Christmas before I didn't get nothin'. I was real mad. It seemed like everybody forgot me. It was the worst Christmas I'd ever had. I cried that whole Christmas long. My aunt got me two pairs of socks. Period. I got everybody a present and nobody got me nothin'. So I made sure that for the bicentennial Christmas I got it all, you know. The store, Wilson's, over there on Golf Road, was goin' outta business, 'n my godmother took me over there with my money from my paycheck to buy all kinds of dresses and skirts and pants and sweaters. I got a beautiful white sweater."

She stares at her hands resting on the table and then looks at me.

"Anyways, I was runnin' up them stairs to get my coat and my new clothes as everyone's runnin' down. Then, with all of them yellin' at me 'Get my coat! Get my shoes!' I sorta forgot what I had come up there to do. They all had blue parkas, so I threw 'em all down. My mother hollered for me to get her house shoes and her boots. It was freezing out there. Eighteen firemen had to go to the hospital. I didn't know who's stuff was who's, I was just grabbin' and throwin'. I put on my sister's shoes, she put on mine. I didn't mind gettin' everybody's stuff, but at least someone could have helped me, y'know?

"Then as I was headed back up the stairs I heard the radiator bangin', it wasn't tingling no more. Then this fireman snatches me from behind, sayin', 'You can't go up them stairs! The whole house is on fire!' I said, 'But my clothes! My clothes!' I tried to break away from him. But even me bein' a tomboy and willful weren't enough for me to do that. All I could think of was my clothes. Most of them was burned. The rest was ruined by smoke inhalation. After that, the family split up and spread out, livin' in two or three different places." She sighs. "After that things never were quite the same."

II

Gwen speaks to me on a hot July afternoon. In a few hours she will go to work where she is a hostess at an Italian restaurant. I meet Gwen at the home of her boyfriend, Jason, and his family. Gwen has been living in this large, two-story, brick house for over six months. Although she is glad to be with Jason, their living arrangements, a room in the basement built with curtains for walls, and her relationship with his mother, trouble her continually.

Because Jason is at the fast-food restaurant his family owns, working one of his three part-time jobs, Gwen has asked me to drive her and her fourteen-month-old daughter, Lashawna, to Evanston Hospital. Lashawna has an appointment to have her ears pierced.

We talk in the living room before leaving.

"When I got pregnant, I was determined to break a family tradition. I made up my mind *I* was going to raise my baby, *not* my grandmother. My grandmother raised nearly everyone of us. See, both my parents booked up on us when I was three, leavin' us with her. That was just before my fourth birthday. And my aunt, see, she's an alcoholic. She didn't even take care of her own kids. She got her alimony check and was always off with that man or this man, you name it. She had so many drunks in her life it isn't even funny. So, my grandmother took care of her kids, too. She put the clothes on our backs, or my cousin's father'd help out. Sometimes some of their relatives would send over a bag of clothes. Other times we'd go to the Salvation Army. And my grandmother fed us, too."

She pauses.

"Now, my father, I can understand him leavin' us, 'cause, number one, we was living with my mother's mother and not his when my mother booked up on us. And, second, he and my grandmother just did not get along. Like they say, 'If you can't live by nobody's rules, get out.' And since my mother booked up on him, he didn't have nothin' really to be there for. I mean, he had us, but he knew we were in good hands, and plus he was always in trouble with the law, and also his folks are in South Carolina. So he figured, hey, you know, he'd be back to visit us 'n everything. But he went down there and got in trouble and got put in jail. So it's not his fault he was away.

"See he's a bullheaded man, my father. He takes the

law into his own hands. Mr. Law, himself. He was in jail for six years. But it wasn't really his fault bein' as times were back then when if a black man kills a white person, you're definitely going to jail. No matter whose fault it was. He was shot seven times. He had owed twenty dollars to this guy and these two other guys stop him outside of a liquor store sayin', 'I hear you owe Big Daddy some money.' He said, 'Look, I pay him when I got the money.' All of a sudden they started pullin' guns on him and firing up. He had got shot a couple of times. Then the lady in the store comes out firing and shot him in his leg. He ran for her, grabbed her gun, shot her while he was still bein' shot a few more times. He had shot and killed two white people; the lady and the storekeeper.

"But he lived. Even with seven holes in him, he was walking home, bleedin' his heart out all over the street. Staggering and shit. He's very, very tough. He's got enough marks on him to last him a lifetime! The police tried to pick him up for drunkenness because of how he was staggering. After they took him to the hospital, he want to jail. Straight up. Six years. Now he's a construction worker. Boy, has he got a life story to tell. He even wrote a book about himself since he was a small child in South Carolina. Being in jail for all them years, I guess you find something to do. The book is real neat; even has all the letters we wrote him while he was in jail.

"He did come up to visit when I was seven months pregnant. My grandmother had him come out to talk to me 'cause I was pregnant and living with Jason. I didn't even know he was coming. He calls me on the phone from the house sayin', 'Hi Gwen.' I say, 'Who's this?' He says, 'You don't know who this is?' I say, 'No!' He says, 'It's your father!' When I found out what he had come for, we had a confrontation. I don't know what he figured he was supposed to do when he got out here. But I told him straight up, 'Look, you've been out of my life since I was four years old, what makes you think you can come back years later and try to tell me how to run my life?' "

Gwen picks gym shoes off the floor and begins to put them on.

"I haven't seen him since. He came all this way to give me a lecture. He sat Jason down and stuck it to him. Callin' him 'boy' 'n everything. Even though I had tried to explain to Jason what kind of man my father is he scared Jason. My father's just a hard man. Stone hard. Like nothing-can-hurt-you hard. Got no feeling about nothing." She sighs as she brushes her hair from the side of her face. "It's just the way he grew up.

"My mother, though, she's got no excuse for her bein' away. She just booked up. Didn't even say good-bye. I mean, if she was in jail or something I could understand. But she's not. After she left, she'd talk to us over the phone and she'd be crying, 'Oh, I miss you all.' Blah, blah, blah."

Gwen's tone is sarcastic.

"She lives in California now. We sorta gotta force her to come here. She was here when we had the fire, and then again around when Lashawna was born. She'll stay a month or so when she comes. But basically, she doesn't like to. My grandmother gives her the real pity trip, 'Oh, if I die soon, what are you gonna do about your kids?' So she comes out of, you know, reluctance. Thing is, once she gets out here, she treats us like she's been out here all her life and everything's fine. But, hey, I don't mind it. I enjoy her bein' out here.

"In fact I talked to her a few months ago and I said, 'Hey, but it's not the fact whether you like it out here, you're coming to visit us. I'm just happy when you're here. So what you booked up on us, I'm old now. If I was still a little three year old and you came back to visit, I wouldn't want to see you. Or, if you had left me at birth, I wouldn't want to see you then either. But nobody's gonna tell you, you know, accuse you, of abandoning us.'

"The only thing I didn't appreciate is when she had another baby out there in California after she left five of us behind."

She raises her arms in exasperation.

"It's like c'mon, ma! But, you know, I'm grown now. She can do whatever she wants. I have a daughter of my own."

Gwen walks into a bedroom off the living room where Lashawna has been sleeping. She wakes her daughter, changes her diaper and then carries her back into the living room. Lashawna seems still to be half asleep. She looks at me. I smile. She buries her head in her mother's neck.

"I don't let my grandmother take care of Lashawna. When she says, 'Oh, I just wish I could stay home and take care of that baby,' I say, 'Oh, no!' One day my grandmother was home 'n on the phone. I told her to watch Lashawna for just a second while I run to the store. She said, 'Are you coming back?' I said, 'No, grandma, I'm gonna stay at the store all night long!' What did she think, I was my mother or something?

When I got back, Lashawna was crying. She'd been playing with one of the pictures on the table and my grandmother took it from her and she didn't like that. My older sister said, 'Hey, Grandma, can't you keep kids under control like you used to?'

"No way, Dan," she says, shaking her finger at me, "I don't trust nobody really with my baby, except maybe my brother. Ask the people at Our Place! People were always wantin' to hold her and play with her. When I'd go to the store I'd take her with me. It's not that I'm overprotective or nothin', it's just that she's going with me."

We walk out the front door, Gwen holding Lashawna in one arm, locking the door with the other. I had parked in front of the house.

"Up at Our Place I never really talked with people about my changes. In some ways it feels like home. People are real friendly, sayin', 'How are you and the baby!' 'What's new?' 'Would you like something?' 'Would you do me a favor?' But I'm one of those people who doesn't get into other people's business and I don't want them gettin' into mine. If it was something real important, well, that's another matter. I usually keep to myself and just get done what I have to get done and enjoy things. I associate with people, but that's different than them being your friends. Still, it's nice to know Our Place is there in case you need it; and I know it's been good for other girls. I remember I went to Our Place when it first opened. They handed me a little yellow brochure about the center. I threw it away, thinking, 'I got no use for this!' Little did I know that in less than a year I'd be comin' here," she says, laughing, as I begin to drive.

"The free public health clinic for teens they got up at the center is good. I know lots of girls who don't think so, though. These pregnant girls are afraid to go up to the clinic. They bad-mouth the place, sayin', 'I'm not going up to that Our Place health-food, health-clinic place. That place's all jive.' But let me tell you somethin' about black people. They're poor and they don't want to call extra attention to this fact. If you go to the free health clinic, it means you can't afford the eighty dollar visits to Evanston Hospital. Well, I'm a lot more practical than that. I'll take anything that's free. It's not a question of pride. I want my daughter to grow up feeling good about herself and her family. It's simply that I'm being realistic about my situation. If there's a good public health clinic that's free, I'll use it. If someone wants to give me some nice hand-me-down clothes for my baby, I'll gladly accept. If I don't have the money to buy my daughter some brand new clothes, I'll go to thrift stores and buy several things when if it was new I could only buy one.

"You see, I had to be realistic all my life. And I've always been sorta independent. I don't have nobody to pay my bills or expenses. When I was eleven I asked my grandmother one day at the laundry mat, 'Lend me a dime.' She said, 'Child, you want a dime, you get yourself a job and earn one.' From that day on I've always worked. I'm not like some teen mothers whose mommy or daddy are still paying their bills. My grandmother doesn't support me financially at all.

"But my grandmother taught me some important things. She taught me at a young age to get things done now, not later and to do them yourself and not to rely on anyone else 'cause if you really need somebody and that person can't be there for you, you're sunk, on your own without a choice. So it makes sense to rely on yourself 'cause in the end, Dan, you're all you've got."

She pauses. I catch a glimpse of Gwen combing Lashawna's hair as I make a right-hand turn.

"I'll bet you're shocked by what I say. No offense, Dan, but white people are always surprised at how much a young black person has experienced; how many of life's responsibilities we often take on while we're young.

"I remember I went to this camp in the summer. It had real log cabins. You name it, they had it. And we had to do chores everyday, and I hated it. Cleaning the bathrooms, mopping the floors, sweeping, all kinds of stuff. Just like home. Now, this camp was mainly black. And there was this white girl in my cabin who said she couldn't sweep. I said, 'Well, who cleans *your* house?' She goes, 'We got a maid.' I go, 'You ain't got one now!' She didn't know how to sweep a broom to save her life. She didn't know how to mop either. And forget dusting! I went to the counselor and said, 'Where did you get this kid?'

"I was so surprised, you know. Thinking from where I grew up, I didn't realize that not everybody knew how to clean. I mean, we were already ten or eleven at the time. I'll tell you, I'm glad I did learn when I was little. 'Cause it looks really weird to see someone that age not knowing how to sweep.

"Maybe I've just always been ahead of other kids my age. I used to be a tomboy. I still like playin' football with the boys. 'Cause I was a quick runner, and quick at schoolwork, the kids called me 'fasty.' My grand-mother said I was, you know, runnin' with the boys.

She always thought I was up to no good. When I got a little older, like in high school, my grandmother'd come to me talkin' all this gossip about me bein' pregnant. She said it to me one day after school. I said, 'What!' She goes, 'I'm fixin' to send you to your mother.' This same thing happened twice. Once she had sent me to the doctor. I didn't know why, 'cause I had already had a physical checkup."

We sit at a red light.

"Somebody at church had told her I was pregnant. Church is where all the gossip is. The gospel of gossip, you might say," she says with a laugh.

"I made the doctor tell me why I was comin' up to the hospital. He told me about my grandmother and the gossip. Thing was, I wasn't sexually active at the time. Heck no. I was too busy bein' a tomboy to think about goin' to bed with somebody. She had sent me, fourteen, and my sister, twelve. Some ol' lady at church had also told her my little sister was on pills. That girl's is no more sexually active than I was then. Victims of gossip. I know why all them old ladies go to church. They're not going to hear the Good Word, they're going to hear the 'good word.' "

Green light.

"When I was thirteen, I knew my mind was ahead of my body. I knew what was going on out there beyond my grandmother's gate. My body was behind the gate, but my mind knew what was on the outside. And I knew to be careful. I knew I should be lookin' to avoid those sweet-talkin', pimpin' young boys. I knew that there was a heck of a lot more to a relationship between a boy and a girl than just a penis and a vagina. I knew there was a lot more to learn than just that. So I'd tell the little boys from the street life to keep on moving 'n not stop in front of my grandmother's gate. I knew then that when I had a baby it would be with the man I had decided to step with; I'd know the man who's the father of my baby, and he'd know he's the father as well.

"Like I said, I was different than most other kids. What I was doin' when I was younger was like an unordinary child. The kids my age was always partyin', gettin' high, hangin' out with boys on the street. I was playin' softball. I mean, I went to parties off and on. I ain't gonna say I never been to a party. But it wasn't my thing. My thing was not to hang out in the streets. Still, my grandmother'd always accuse me of bein' out all the time." She sighs. "Well, I guess that's true. I didn't like stayin' in that house because she was there, number one. So I always stayed outside the house, okay? I was fourteen and I had a boyfriend. He was as much an athlete as I was. We was always out playin' basketball with my two sisters, or football, softball or we were bike-riding down at the beach. We were always out doing something.

"So I don't know what my grandmother was thinkin' or gossipin' about. Once I overheard my grandmother on the phone telling somebody I was a whore. I figured if it's not true, it's not true. She used to make me cry when she'd accuse me of hangin' out on the streets. I figured why should I sit here and cry my eyes out if it's not true. I decided, shoot, she can think that if she wants to, but tough, it's not true, so I'd better just get on with what I was doin'. And besides since the fire there was only one TV at home and the rule was the first one to turn it on got to watch whatever he wanted to. So I'd just go over to my boyfriend's house. Hey, they had a TV practically in every room in that house. If I didn't like what they were watchin' on one TV, I'd get the one in the next room. I wasn't off runnin' in the streets. I just like to go do things I enjoyed doin'.''

Gwen stares out the window. Lashawna rests in her mother's arms. I see the hospital a few blocks ahead.

"That's why I got mad at this one doctor I had when I was gettin' a checkup when I was pregnant. He was sayin' how most blacks should give up their kids or have an abortion and that fifteen was too young of an age to have kids, that I should be thinkin' about my future, what I'm gonna be doin' four and five years from now with all these kids runnin' around. He said, 'Just think of how your life is gonna be when you're young and you can't have all the fun other young people have.' Thing is, I never had fun like other kids did anyway. Bein' a parent hasn't taken away any freedom I had. I never really did anything in the first place besides goin' to school, workin', playin' a bit, and sleepin'.

"One day we had this same talk at Our Place with the Partners. They were all tellin' us how it was when they were teens. I said, 'Hey, any place I want to go and I feel that Lashawna can go with me, I go.' They got the wrong idea. They thought, 'You mean if you want to go to a party you gonna bring Lashawna with you?' I'm like, 'Funny.' I'm laughin' at this. I said. 'For number one, like I don't go to parties. If I go, so what? The only party I've been to was a birthday party. It was Lashawna's godmother's birthday. So I brought her and she slept through the whole thing. Hey, I don't put my burden on nobody. If I feel I have somewhere to go and I can't bring her, well, I don't go. It hasn't happened yet. But my brother's always callin' to see if I need him to watch the baby. If he offers, fine. But I won't ask nobody for nothin'; except for when I have to go to work. But I'd never ask anyone to sit for her so I can go out for my own personal pleasure."

Gwen talks as I park the car.

"And I hate it when people ask me, 'Do you ever wish you weren't a parent? It's just not right to ask a question like that. That's like askin' me if I want to give Lashawna up, like askin' me if I wish she wasn't alive! I am her mother. I planned to have her. The summer before my junior year in high school, Jason and I drove by car from New York City to Florida with his family. It was on that trip that we picked out names for a child. I wasn't pregnant then. But I was thinkin' about it. I had to make sure he was the man for me. By September I was pregnant. Like I said, I was fifteen, I kept going to school. I even took extra classes so I could graduate early."

Before entering the hospital's front door, Gwen hesitates. Turning to me, she raises her hand as if to offer a toast. She has a wry smile.

"Here's to all those doctors and teachers who said I couldn't raise a baby at my age, let alone graduate from school early. I had to prove to all of them, my grandmother, other teens that not all teens are dumb and ignorant about makin' good choices for themselves. I love proving people wrong. I was gonna be a good example. I knew all about raising children. I had stored up in me all this knowledge about babies and with my own baby I felt I could apply it to my own instead of always telling others what I know. When I was seven, my cousins were having babies. I've been around babies all my life. I'm still the same person I was before I was a parent. Only thing that's changed is that I have a baby. Same ol' me, though.

"And I'm glad I had Lashawna while I am young. I want us to be able to be close in age so when she gets older she won't have an *old* mother, but a young one. That way I can always have the companionship of my daughter. We'll be able to go places and do all kinds of things together. We'll be real close."

I ask, "How would you feel if Lashawna became pregnant when she turns fifteen or sixteen?"

"Well," she sighs, "I guess I'll become a grand-mother then. And I guess I'll try and do her better than was done to me, you know."

"Really? You wouldn't be angry at her?"

"No, Dan, you see, that's the thing these days. More and more young girls are realizing that they don't want to be real old when their children are growing up. You see, if I'm thirty-two when my daughter is sixteen, then I won't be so much older than her and she won't think her mother's out of reach. A girl I know, her parent's are about fifty-five or sixty or sixty-five or whatever. They're so old it makes her feel like they can't under-stand her. And I don't want my daughter to feel that way about me."

Down a long corridor, we walk toward the Child and Adolescent Center.

"When I was pregnant I thought of my mother a lot, like when she was pregnant with me. There was a lot I wanted to ask her, you know, like how she felt then, what I was like as a tiny little infant, what were her feelings about being a teen mother. You see, we were both mothers at sixteen. Weird, eh? She had her first child, though, when she was thirteen.

"But she wasn't around for me to ask, so I'd have to ask my grandmother. But she wasn't any help. She'd say, 'It wasn't *me* that was your mommy.''

She sighs.

"Someday Lashawna will have a brother or sister. Two, though will be enough. But I'm just thinkin' about it." She laughs nervously. "That's all, just thinkin' about it. Jason keeps goin', 'When's the little boy comin'? When's the little boy comin'?' So, I'm just thinkin' about it."

She giggles and shrugs her shoulders.

"I really don't know. It won't be no five years, though. It depends. Depends on how I feel."

We turn a corner. She is quiet. She shakes her head.

"Thing is, birth control," she says abruptly. "At the clinic they told me I couldn't use pills. So I'm stuck with whatever I got and I don't use nothin'. I've been through a year safely, so you know, it's weird. I mean, I was sexually active for a whole entire year, and then I had her, okay? And then after having her, it's been a year and still I haven't got pregnant." She pauses. "I guess I'm fortunate. I figure if I do get pregnant, goody-woody, here comes a kid. I'd just like to be prepared for it, that's all. Like financially. I got medical insurance for it and everything.

"My grandmother keeps thinkin' me and Jason should get married and get ourselves an apartment and settle down. You know the rap. Anyways, I know I wasn't ready for marriage when I got pregnant, and I'm not now. Deep down inside I just know it. I can't quite tell you why, but I know it. Besides, I don't think I ever want to get married. Oh, I'll be with Jason, all right. But not married. Not me," she laughs. "I'm a liberated woman!"

III

Bored, angry, and tired, Gwen goes for a walk. I walk with her. It's cold and gray. It's January. It's thirty below zero.

We walk west on Dempster, her regular route. I am surprised at our quick pace. In a week, Gwen is due to give birth to her second child.

"The pregnancy is much different than the first. With my first, I was always in the public eye. It was new, I had lots of energy, people came around to see me all the time. I felt good. I was in school. I was getting lots of exercise, walking, climbing stairs. My back never hurt.

"Now I just sit at home with Lashawna when I'm not at work. My friends, my so-called friends, don't return my calls. I've been real down. Bitchy and mean, causing fights with Jason. Never used to be like that. My back hurts, that's one reason I gotta walk. Can't stand sitting still. When I was pregnant with Lashawna I was always happy, at least it seemed so. Now, I just rush this pregnancy. Just want it to be over. Hurry up and give me something to do!

"You know, I walk down Dempster when I'm upset. Walked it the night I told Jason I was pregnant again. I waited till I was four and half months pregnant. I was sorta scared to tell him, but I wanted to surprise him, too. He'd been asking about that little boy for so long. Then one night while we was arguing about something, don't ask me what it was, maybe I don't remember 'cause I don't want to. Remembering is like how old people hear: you only hear what you want to hear!" She laughs. "So in the middle of us quarreling, I just sorta tell him. Didn't intend to, especially in the middle of a fight. But I was upset.

"He said he wasn't ready to have another baby. He's telling me he's ready to marry me, but not ready to have my baby. Heck, *our* baby! I was so mad I told him. 'I wouldn't marry you if you paid me!' I also told him if he wasn't going to stand by me, I was going to leave. Only then did it become real to him that I was really pregnant again.

"Thing is, we wanted two kids. We've had lots of talks since then. I'm going to use birth control now."

She is quiet. We walk. My beard and mustache have frozen.

She smiles.

"Not too long after I decided Jason was the man for me, we started sleeping together. He'd sneak over to my grandmother's at night, then in the morning he'd sneak back out real early before my grandmother'd go to work at six o'clock and my aunt at seven thirty. We had rigged up this system of him climbing out of the bedroom window onto a shed where we'd keep two wood crates for steps. One morning, though, I heard my grandmother come upstairs to my room before she went to work. Jason jumped up and tried to open the window but the ice had frozen it shut. Just when we thought we'd be caught, it opened and out he went! When my grandmother came in, I told her the window was stuck and I was trying to close it all the way. She came back with some of that big heavy tape and sealed that window up tight. Well, as you can tell, that ended our sleeping there."

After a pause, she begins to hum a tune.

"I always liked that song. It's usually for little kids at church. It's called, 'What Did You Do with Your Life Today?' It goes, 'What did you do with your life today?

Did you use it wisely, or throw it away? It's a precious gift that you did not earn, or that you didn't have to go to school to learn. Do you remember what you did? How you did it? When you did it? Where you did it? What did you do with your life today?'

"And that's just the thing. Some people don't know what they did today or yesterday: 'I don't know. I forgot.' For me, most of the songs I like ask questions. To make me think. I enjoy a lot of music. But mainly I listen to music that speaks about myself. I try and ask myself what did I do with my life today? But these things seem like a waste. Being lonely and bored isn't doin' much with my life. I'm not even praying as much as I usually do. When I was pregnant with Lashawna I'd pray all the time for my baby to be all right and healthy. I don't even read my Bible or go to church like I used to. I feel like I'm slippin' backwards. I love to sing. And I pray for the strength to get back into that routine. You see, singin' is my true craving. But I haven't had it in me. It's nobody's fault but mine. I'll make plans to go to choir rehearsal and then something will happen and I'll miss out. It won't slip my mind on purpose. I'll just realize I had forgot later on. And I'll feel kinda bad, 'cause I want to do it, no one's keepin' me from doin' it, it's just that I ain't done it yet. Been too bored."

Gwen pulls her scarf over her mouth.

"I'll say one thing for Jason," she says in a muffled tone, "if he didn't love me, I wouldn't be here. That's one thing everybody'll say, even my whole family: 'One thing about that ol' Jason, he sure in the hell loves you.' Say I go somewhere and he don't know where I'm at, he'll scout the whole of Evanston for me. Then the next day when people see me, they'll say, 'I hope Jason found you, 'cause he came to my house three times lookin' for you! At least he cares about you. With some men, if you ain't home, tough!' "

We walk a block without talking.

I ask, "And you, how do you feel about Jason? Do you love him?"

She laughs.

"All afternoon I was afraid you were going to ask me that question! I told you six months ago, that's one topic I won't talk about. Just prefer not to. I guess in my family we never talked much about love. I'll talk about anything else you want to. Just don't ask me about love."

Hunger

Verlene Moore takes a bite from a taffy apple. She had unwrapped it even before she walked through the front door. She sits next to me on a couch in the hallway. At sixteen, Verlene has not been in school in over a year.

"Lord, I am hungry!" she says between bites. "I've got one big appetite. Always have. I love to eat. All kinds of food. Junk food, mostly. Cheeseburgers, fries, chips. Even like greens. Anything."

She talks as she chews. "I've always been a big eater, but I guess 'specially so 'cause of my baby. Bein' pregnant makes me hungrier."

"How many months have you been pregnant?" I ask.

"Could be one month, two, maybe even three. I don't really know."

She shrugs her shoulders.

She has a trace of a smile.

She continues to chew.

"How do you feel about being pregnant?"

"It's sorta nice 'n all. But to tell you the truth, scary. I feel real scared. I ain't never been pregnant before. My two sisters has, they got kids. But not me. This is my first time. See, my friend, Nora, she was sixteen just like me, she died last week from some kind of problems havin' to do with bein' pregnant and havin' babies. Bleedin' or somethin'. I don't want that to happen to me, you understand. Yeah. Not to me. I feel fear, all right."

Verlene opens a bag of barbequed potato chips.

"I'm hopin' for a boy, though. I want him to look just like his daddy. Oh, Lord, is that man fine! Beautiful, long, full hair. Nice complexion. Tall. Yeah. Just like his daddy. That's what I want. Lord, that man is fine!"

She can't hide her smile.

"He's kinda my boyfriend, I know him real well. He's older 'n me. I didn't intend on havin' this baby, though. But, you know how things can happen. It just happened. Anyways, he's got eight other kids, 'n I know the mothers of each of 'em.

"Want a potato chip?"

Innocence

Yvonne Packer sits at a sewing machine. Christine, her seventeen-month-old daughter, sits in her lap. Yvonne is making a dress.

"When I had Christine, I had just turned sixteen. I didn't know nothin' about babies. Not one thing. Didn't even know how to hold one. The nurse at the hospital had to show me so I could try 'n nurse her properly. Would you believe my ol' man had to tell me I was pregnant! I mean, I knew somethin' was up, but I didn't know what exactly. Oooo, I was doin' crazy things I ain't never done before! Puttin' syrup on cereal, ketchup on pickles, chili powder on chili, peanut butter on bananas. I just had this fierce cravin' to eat. My boyfriend said, 'Girl, I'd better take you up to the hospital to get yourself checked out!'

"There's still a whole lot I gotta learn 'bout babies. I had read this article in one of them baby magazines they've got here at the center. It was all about a baby's first year of life. All kinds of neat pictures of babies walkin' and crawlin'. It really showed me a lot. I showed it to the other girls in the child development class."

Yvonne pauses to examine her work. The hem is nearly complete.

"I remember the night Christine was born. I was watching a TV show called *Having Babies*. It was a good show. Just so happened that night my water bag broke. I was feelin' real funny, I started hurtin' real bad. Water started runnin' all down the inside of my legs 'n onto the floor. It was real awful. It really upset me. I knew it was gonna happen, I knew that much. But I just wasn't ready for it to happen right then and there. Once my bag broke, I sure knew what was goin' on! I knew my baby was comin'! My cousin fixed the flat tire on the car and my sister rushed over to the emergency room. I was lyin' on the floor squirmin' and screamin'! Ooooooo! It was awful!

"What made matters worse was I was still mad at my ol' man. He had made all these big promises, 'Yvonne, I'll do this for you and that for you and the baby, too.' He said he was gonna marry me, too. He left when I was four months pregnant. If it wasn't for all his talkin' and promisin' I'd a gotten an abortion or maybe put my baby up for adoption. No joke. Just thinkin' about him makes me sick. I guess I was also sorta mad at myself, Dan, for allowin' him to have that kind of influence over me."

With a hug, Yvonne leans over and kisses Christine on her head.

The Kitchen

I sit with several teens in the front of the parents'
room. The staff is meeting with a young mother in the
back, near the kitchen.

Kendra Jackson enters the parents' room already
complaining. "They's always up there! They's always
meetin' with some troubled person or another. Man,
we can never get up in there! That kitchen's always off
limits for one damn reason or another."

"That's right!" a voice agrees.

"I swear!" says another.

Carla Griffiths stands up. "Y'all don't know what
you're talkin' about. People's got troubles. These people here are just tryin' to help some people out. You
don't know what kind of trouble people's got! Y'all
think you're so high and mighty sittin' up here thinkin'
you're superior to others. Yeah, you've got this nice
center to come to but don't forget y'all isn't the only
ones up in here. Just 'cause some folks don't think so
high and mighty of themselves to tell their problems,
doesn't mean you all can talk down about them."

"Well, that may be so, but they still could have their
meetings at some other time when we need to get in
there!" Kendra says. "That kitchen is for everyone,
y'know."

Carla puts her hands on her hips.

"You silly dames don't know shit," she says. "You don't have no kind'a idea what this place is doin' for some people. People can't just choose when they're gonna have a serious problem, y'know. That poor girl in there didn't plan to have her a problem just so you couldn't get in that kitchen."

Carla looks first at Kendra and then at the others.

"Y'all is terrible! They're people who don't have the tight families y'all prob'ly come from. Our Place is a good place 'cause it's here for people like me who don't have no regular family to go home to every night, so I come here nearly every day. It helps people like me from stayin' off the street. Folks here offer folks the help they need."

She points to a photograph of the staff that hangs on the wall. "I mean, I can come in here and choose any one of those six people who want to help me, who ain't those white social workers who just hassle the hell outta you.

"Look," she says in a calmer voice, "I know what I'm talkin' about. I had me two kids and you can see where I am with my third. No one's paid me this much attention ever. Folks here are tryin' to help me get my GED. I tried stayin' in school like some of you all but that didn't last passed ninth grade. Shit, my grandmother done took my two other kids and I lost one in a miscarriage. Thank the Lord, I was able to have me one more, conceived on my birthday, mind you. But I can see now, this one's my last. After this one, I'm havin' my tubes tied. No more babies, no more accidents for me," she says with a smile.

Kendra laughs.

Carla's calm disappears. She points a finger at Kendra and yells, "So don't be all high 'n mighty 'round me, honey! These folks are tryin' to help me get things together so's I can do right by my child!"

Carla walks toward the door. "Shit, y'all think trouble's when you're kept from going *in* the kitchen."

The Table

Howard Nathaniel Manning has just had his breakfast. On this February morning there is a chill in the dining room of the apartment where he lives. Howard sits in a high chair, wears a bib with a bear embroidered on it, and drinks from his bottle. Howard is ten months old.

His mother, Sandra, sits with me at the dining room table. She is older than the other girls at the center. At twenty, she has been a high school graduate for two years. Although Sandra and Howard live with her girl friend, Lynn, Lynn's two-year-old son, Kenneth, and Lynn's mother, Mrs. Florence Clemons, they have their own mailbox: Sandra and Howard Manning.

"So you want to write about me in a book?" Sandra says as she paints her fingernails. "Well, I'm twenty years old. I have a beautiful baby. I went to Martin Luther King, Jr., Lab School, Nichols School, St. Ann's High School, and Evanston Township High School. I worked at Brown's Chicken and then at Kraft Foods for almost two years. Then I got pregnant and here I am."

She holds out her hand to examine her work.

"Well, Dan, I guess that's what my life's been about. So, what else do you want to know about me?"

She laughs.

I remember the day Sandra was due to give birth to Howard. She had lifted the bottom of her shirt to show some of the girls at Our Place her taut and firm stomach. She seemed relaxed and they were laughing. She looked down at her bulging stomach and said to her unborn child: "You get outta there! This is your eviction notice. Your rent is overdue and it's time for you to move out!" They laughed. "I'll be going to the hospital when I feel the big kick five big times in one hour, but not a minute sooner. I don't want to sit around there and hear all those mothers wailin' 'n screamin', makin' me all nervous and unsettled. I'm gonna have my baby in no time flat, spend one or two nights in the hospital, and then slide on home to my mother's."

Sandra then asked me if I wanted to feel her baby moving inside her. I put my hand on her stomach. I felt it tighten and twitch. It was the first time I had ever felt a pregnant woman's stomach.

"No, seriously, did you know I almost didn't become a parent. That's right. I almost gave my baby up for adoption. I got pregnant by accident. You know, just foolin' around with my boyfriend. That's the problem with the rhythm method. You got to be in control at all times. We was both real high. Bein' pregnant at first brought me real down. Usually I'm pretty good at handling changes, but when I started to carry my load, well, let me put it to you this way, bein' pregnant took me through some changes. Everything happened to me all at once. My girl friend and I had just been evicted because she couldn't pay her share of the rent. Then my mother moved out of Evanston, leavin' me all by myself in some little room I found. I'd been working for almost two years and I hadn't got a bonus in all that time. I ended up getting in a fight with my supervisor and getting fired. I was tired of that ol' job anyways. No bonus after all that time. Just wasn't worth it to me. And to top it off, I got pregnant.

"I'm not afraid to say it was a bad time for me. Our Place really helped me through a lot of heavy shit. I even got a CETA job working at Our Place after my baby was born. I knew about Our Place 'cause I remember it used to be the C and W restaurant. It was the only restaurant open at two o'clock in the morning when I'd be hungry! At first, I'd come around Our Place just to see what was up. I was going crazy in my little room. Do you know what it's like to be all locked up in a tiny ol' room with no one to talk to and nothin' to do but watch the soaps on TV? I woulda had me an abortion but I waited too long. That's how I started thinkin' about givin' up my baby.

"But after I started coming up to Our Place and seeing how those other girls were doing, and how they was all younger 'n me, I told myself that I could do it, too. The girls would talk to me and tell me that they had lots of problems, too. And no one hassled me 'cause I was pregnant. You could talk and listen and share your problems, do things with them, and just be with people, laughing about whatever, and learning about your baby and yourself. And once someone said to me, 'When you see your baby, you won't want to give him up.' She was right."

She looks at Howard drinking his milk. "For the last year or so I've ended up talking about child care and parenting and babies and myself about three times a week. I'd go to the child development workshops, I was in Partners, and I was going to my prenatal class at Evanston Hospital. I knew a lot about kids before I had one. Shit, I used to have to watch and take care of five or six kids at a time when I used to baby-sit. So havin' a baby is really no big thing. I still have lots of time for myself, only now I have to be more efficient with it. It used to take me a while to clean him, but now I've got it down. I wash him in warm water and change his diapers, and then I clean and comb his hair, wash the insides of his ears and then the insides of his nose; all in about ten or fifteen minutes at most. Then I get myself showered and dressed, get my son fed and dressed, and straighten up the house in no time. Bein' a mother even enhanced my social life! And one way or another I still find time to do my nails."

She speaks with confidence. Sandra likes me to see how she's been able to keep things under control. I remember the tour of the apartment she'd given me when I had arrived. "See how clean everything is. We always keep it this way," she had said, pointing to a room. "That's where Lynn's mother sleeps. She's got the big bed and the color TV. And this here's me and Lynn's room. But it's no big thing, only one bed, 'cause at least one of us is usually out for the night anyways," she had said with a smile. "If we're both here, the couch in the living room folds out. So you see, Dan, everything's cool. I pay Florence my little rent, and everything's cool. Only thing she don't allow is us bringin' men around her place."

She continues to speak. "I got four godmothers, not one like most folks. And I've got a lot of family, too. And anyone of 'em would take Howard for weeks if I wanted 'em to. That's the truth, too. Thing is, even with all this help, I'm too independent to want to rely on my family for everything.

"My family's done right by me. We always had plenty of money, not like my cousins who lived in the projects. And I've been all over, too. My godfather took me to California, Florida, Mississippi, Sweden, and France. That's right, I've been to Europe, too. But since I need my independence from my family, Our Place is cool, y'know, 'cause it's sorta like a family, but it's not.

"Anyways, my family sent me to this religious school in Mississippi 'cause they thought I was acting too uppity and wild. I liked the school down there. We'd party and shit. My family sent me there to learn some discipline and obedience. But for me, it just got me away. I was a model student: class secretary, president of the choir club, class president my senior year. But I got thrown out for smokin' a little reefer. I still can't even smoke a regular ol' cigarette in front of my mother without her going crazy. I bet when I'm thirty I'll still be too afraid to. See, she's a churchwoman and I'm what you call a sinner woman. I like to drink and smoke and have a good time."

She tilts her head to one side and raises her eyebrows.

"But she's only got herself to blame. When I was sixteen, I wanted to go back to church with her, but she wouldn't let me 'cause of me bein' kicked outta school. I'd been a churchgoer when I was a little girl, but I stopped going. To this day I tell her she shoulda let me go when I wanted to. Now she wishes I'd go more.

"But I'm gonna do things different with my son. I'm gonna take him to church, or let his godmother take him. I want him to know about God and religion and all. And I'm gonna give my son more freedom, too. I'll buy him whatever he needs. If he wants to go to college, fine. I'll help him out with tuition and spending money or a car or whatever. But if he does that, he'll have to accept the responsibility of doing all the work. If he doesn't want to go to college and he wants to stay around here, he'll have to support himself. I'll feed him, but if he wants to party and go out and stuff, well, that's a different story. He'll have to finance his own habits."

Her hands lay flat on the table. Her fingers are spread out to let the nail polish dry.

"Actually, now that I'm a parent I can better appreciate what my mother went through. Shit, she had my brother in 1959, me in 1960, my other brother in 1962, and my little sister in 1965. All of us to take care of. All I can say is diapers, diapers, diapers! But not me. I'm gonna just have my son and that's all." She pauses. "Maybe I'll have another baby, a girl, in five or six years. But he's all I can handle for now.

"Besides, I don't like having my stomach all stretched out of shape, leaving you with them nasty ol' stretch marks. My poor body went through too many changes while I was pregnant. I remember a few days after Howard was born, my legs were still shaking and I couldn't stop 'em. The nurse said it was 'cause giving birth puts the mother's body through a lot of stress, sort of shocking the whole system. Shoot, Dan, just 'cause I've got my hair looking nice, some makeup on, some nice clothes and all, doesn't mean I've recovered one hundred percent!"

She crosses her legs.

"But one thing I'll never do is get married. No way. Too much divorce in my family. My mother's been divorced twice, my uncle twice, my grandmother twice. I've learned that marriage just doesn't work. I'll have plenty of boyfriends, but no husbands. Women got to be careful of men. The reason I don't let my baby's father see our son is because he's not helpin' support him financially. If the father wants rights, he's got to live up to his responsibilities. No responsibilities, no rights. I won't let no man just barge in here and start ordering me around whenever he damn please. Not with me. I'm not one of those girls! No man's gonna beat me or push me around. My girl friend couldn't say no to her boyfriend and I found her all bloody and beat up with her blouse torn off. Any man who raises a hand to me is gone, and I mean fast!"

Her voice had become louder, more adamant.

"I've just seen too much fightin' and screamin' in my day to go lookin' for more of it. That's why I like to have the rent lease in my name, so no man can tell me to up and move. You bet, I'm gonna stay independent. Just me and my sweet man, Howard."

She touches his cheek with the back of her hand and then puts his empty bottle on the table.

"Isn't he beautiful?" she sighs. "Looks just like his daddy. Real light-skinned. My daddy's real dark. Y'know when Martin Luther King was shot, that's when I learned about racial prejudice and stuff. White kids at school were callin' us niggers. I remember runnin' home crying, 'Mama, Mama, what's a nigger?' Ooooo, I was cryin'!

"But color's not a problem with me, though, except

for real black, y'know, blue-black. I just don't like that. For me, the lighter, the better."

She pauses and then sighs again. She slouches in her chair and then looks at her son.

"Yeah, I was real frightened when kids called me nigger. I remember a lot of screamin' and fightin'. Screaming's always upset me. My father was always screamin' and fightin'. I used to have this one nightmare all the time when I was a little girl. I still have it sometimes.

"In this dream there are all these tables and chairs in a large room, like at Woolworth's, downtown. And there's this big wall with wallpaper on it and there was a big hole in it and I'd sit in that hole and look out onto this room with all the tables and chairs. And then I'd hear this big ol' giant monster coming. He was running real, real fast. I'd run under this one table every time hopin' the monster wouldn't get me, wishin' so hard he wouldn't see me, prayin' to God like I'd do when my father'd be chasin' me, tryin' to whup me after he'd been fightin' with my mother."

Sandra's voice had been shaking. Her eyes are closed.

"Y'know, I feel like fightin' right now. I really do. I almost got off into it yesterday. I really felt like jumpin' down this one girl's neck."

Her right hand had become a fist.

Looking at me, she laughs, and with a wink smiles mischievously.

"But, you know me, Dan. I'm still a child in many ways. I still got the child in me somewhere."

Rocking

Moving back and forth, Jeanne Hutton sits in a rocking chair in the child-care room. She wears her winter coat, her arms folded across her chest. She stares down at her feet.

I have known Jeanne for about a year. At sixteen, she is the mother of two-month-old Steven.

She hears my voice in the hall, and she asks me to come in. Usually, she won't talk to me unless she has a friend with her. I sit on a table, my back leaning against a wall, watching her.

"What's up, Jeanne?" I ask.

"Nothing," she answers.

"Nothing?"

"Yeah, nothing. That's just it. Nothin's happenin'. I'm so bored. I'm really bored."

We sit in silence.

She continues to rock.

"Y'know," she says, "I like to go out 'n have fun. I've always been an active person. All this sittin' around isn't for me. I just can't take it. Listenin' to this baby cry all the time, I swear."

She looks at me.

"Do you realize I'm sixteen and I feel like I almost forgot how to party! I mean, forgot how to party! I tell you, I'm too young for that. I didn't do a thing for nine months and my mother still wants me to sit around the house doin' nothin'. I mean, she wants me to keep goin' to school 'n all, but that's boring, too. Well, I'm tired of sittin' around at home and at school. I mean, she ought to give me a month or two to get back into things, you know, to have me some freedom for a while. Then, I can ease back into all this boredom and responsibility.

"I hate to admit it, Dan, but I'm just not cut out for this motherhood stuff. I thought I'd be, but I'm not. Guess I found out too late, huh? I wish I'd had my baby when I was in my late twenties. That woulda given me lots of time to party and run around and have fun. If I knew what I know now, I'da had me an abortion."

Jeanne pauses.

"But I should stop this silly talk. I don't believe in abortions. And besides I love my baby."

She is quiet again.

"My baby's father believes in abortions, but I wanted to have the baby. He said he wanted me to have his baby 'n that he'd stay with me. If it was a boy, he wanted me to name it after him. But long about three months pregnant he started denyin' it was his. I'd be stayin' up late at night cryin'. I wanted him to claim it as his own, you know, publicly. I remember I just couldn't wait to get back at him, to have everyone see how much it would look like him. Then he couldn't deny nothin'!

"Thing was, I'd been usin' birth control all along, up until I thought I was gonna move back south again. I'd stopped using the pill before I was gonna go. By stoppin' usin' the pill I thought I wouldn't, you know, mess around when I left Evanston. Also, I thought it might make Steve respect me more. Well, late one night, you know, in the heat of it, we got into it. We was both high. Thing is, I usually know what I'm doin' when I'm high. Didn't that night, huh? I sure didn't plan on gettin' pregnant, didn't intend to at all.

"When I realized I gave birth to a boy, you know, when the doctor tells you right after the baby comes out of you, I was cryin', cryin' real hard. I was cryin', 'I don't want him! I don't want him! I want a girl, not a boy!' My mother's best friend was with me. She slapped me on the face, 'Girl, don't you talk like that about your child.' I felt so bad. 'Bout fifteen minutes later I was cryin' for the nurse to bring me back my baby. And she did. I really had been hopin' for a girl, though. I really didn't want to name my baby after his father. But I did. At first my baby was all pale and yellow. I didn't think he'd be lookin' like that, so pale. Lately, his color's been changin', though. He's browner than before."

Very slowly, she sighs.

"Thing is, Dan, I'm bored. Sometimes I don't even have the energy to run around if I could. I swear, I wish I was back where I was pregnant again."

"How about before you were pregnant?" I ask.

"Sounds even better. See, I like stayin' out till five o'clock in the mornin'. Once I stayed out till seven o'clock. My mother won't let me do that. I gotta be in by midnight 'cause she don't like baby-sittin' no more 'n I do. If I want to stay out late with no miserable midnight curfew, I take my baby to my grandmother's. She loves to take care of my baby. She loves babies. She doesn't mind. But my mother doesn't like me doin' that.

"Damn, I feel like a slave! All locked up with no freedom of my own. Yeah. A slave all right. Curfews and rules and punishments. No freedom. It's just not fair, Dan. It's not fair that I can't go out, that I got to take care of this screaming, crying baby all day and all night. He's wakin' up all the time now in the middle of the night and it makes me real tired. Last night he woke me up with his cryin'. I just couldn't handle it. I grabbed him 'n put him in bed with my mother. I let her take care of him. I'd had enough.

"His father sure don't come around to baby-sit. I wish he would. It'd give *me* some freedom if he did. But I ain't never known one of 'em to do that for no girl. I don't know how Josie does it with her three kids. I don't know how any of these girls do it even with one kid on their hands. Maybe it's just me, maybe I'm the problem. But I can't help that. I need some freedom. This responsibility is too much for me."

Jeanne rocks in a slow, steady rhythm, still staring at her feet. "I swear, it's like I'm a slave."

What Goes Around,
Comes Around

My little boy, eyes so bright
I'll rock you, I'll love you
I'll care for you tonight

But who's going to care for me?
Who's going to set me free?

Pauline Thompson wrote this poem when she was fifteen. At the time, her son David was already two years old.

Pauline is now twenty-eight, mother of three boys, and married to Eliot Thompson, father of her two youngest children. On the November evening Pauline recites her poem to me, she is six months pregnant with her fourth child.

Pauline's family has lived in Evanston for 128 years. Charles Hewitt, Pauline's great-great-grandfather, came to Evanston from Iowa in 1854. Her father's family has made Evanston its home since the late 1890s. Four generations of her family have graduated from Evanston Township High School. Pauline and Eliot and their children live on the first floor of a house she and her husband have owned for five years. "Make no mistake about it," she says to me, "I'm an Evanstonian from way back."

Pauline plays a special role at Our Place. For two years she and fourteen other adult women have served as "big sisters" to many of the teen mothers who use the center. Through the Partners Program each teen mother (or junior Partner) under the age of seventeen is assigned a "big sister" (a senior Partner) to whom she can turn for support, advice, friendship. Each senior Partner was once a teen parent.

I sit with Pauline on a couch in her living room. Assorted boxes stand piled near the doorway leading to the dining room. Across the room, under the window, is a beige dropcloth covering a small table. Next to the window, a ladder leans against the wall. Beneath the ladder are several jars, a large can of paint remover and a few paint scrapers. Pauline and Eliot have stripped the paint from the woodwork in their living room and dining room. Only the molding above the window needs work.

"I just did it," she says, looking around the room. "I wanted to see that pretty woodwork. I love the grain in that ol' oak and pine. Somehow I find the time for things that are important to me. That's just how I am. If I didn't, I'd be nowhere."

She takes a slow sip from her cup of coffee. "I came from a quiet work-and-come-home Evanston family. I'm pretty much like that today, but I've made some changes. I go to Our Place every Thursday night. Since I'm not at home with my kids on Thursday nights I try to make the other times we have together especially meaningful for all of us. My kids know it's important for me to participate and be a community-oriented person. I want them to know it's possible to be involved and still to have quality relationships. Quantity isn't quality, you might say.

"You see, I'm the kind of person who's got to be growing all the time. And for me, I feel I grow through participation in my community. I work and I have a family. But I've been workin' 'n havin' a family for a long time now. Since I was a child I've learned all the cookin' and cleanin' in the world, but it's become routine. And when things become automatic, it means I'm not growing any more. That's my signal that I've got to move on and branch out some. For me, it's important to be active. Like if I go to a Partners meeting and only one girl asks a question, then I have that question to think on and contemplate. I try to come up with an answer to help that girl who asked the question. Maybe it'll help all the others who were too bashful to ask."

Pauline rests her arm along the back of the couch. "I feel about this house like I feel about Evanston. Both are my home. Home just isn't the walls you live inside of. It's the block your house or apartment is on, it's your neighborhood, it's your kid's school, it's the hospital and it's the parks. I care about the young ones, the children. I know it sounds cliché, but these children are our future. If they got trouble, we all got trouble. If the adults had been paying attention in the first place, the children wouldn't be allowed to get in trouble. We're the ones who should be setting the example for the children.

"This house is always filled with kids from all over the neighborhood. I'll be bakin' them cookies or makin' them pizza. That's their favorite. We'll go to the zoo or the park right there across the street. Once I ended up takin' thirty-five kids to Dominicks with me. The lady at the counter was so amazed she dumped a full tray of suckers in my bag when I was done shoppin'! You got to show kids you care by doin' stuff with them.

"I could be the kind who stays home in the comfort of

my private life. But that's just the problem. I can't. There are just too many people stayin' home, keepin' to themselves. The ol' extended family just isn't extending itself like it used to. What happened to our families is that nothing's happened!" she says as she raises her voice. "That's the problem, that nothing's happened. That's why that place up the street is so important to us. That's why I go to Our Place."

Pauline stretches her legs out across the coffee table. "Something's changed here in Evanston. When I was comin' up things really were different. I know how that sounds, old people were always saying that to me when I was young. But it's really true. Things have changed. See, neighbors used to watch you as if you were their own. If you got out of line and your parents weren't around, the man or lady down the block would discipline you or talk to you right then and there. And you'd stop, too. 'Cause you knew they'd telephone your mother or father, and you knew you'd catch a whuppin' from them when they'd get home!

"No one likes to be disciplined, but back then you had a sense that people cared enough about you to steer you away from trouble. We all knew we had each other. No matter how hard times might be, we always had each other: grandparents, aunts, uncles, cousins, neighbors, and friends.

"Now I've taken my grandmother's position as the center of the family. My whole family calls me if they need something. Even my mother-in-law calls me. Yesterday she wanted me to go out and get her some aspirin. People tell me all the time that their first impression of me is that I'm a tough, mean, ol' independent woman. But, you see, I know I wouldn't be doin' all that if I didn't know that they're are a whole bunch of people who love me, who really love their Pauline. I can tell you straight to your face that I am loved by so many people. My mother loved me, my father loves me, my husband loves me, my children love me.

"Just the other night my father calls me. I pick up the phone and he says, 'Did I wake you, baby?' And I said, 'That's okay.' And he said, 'I won't keep you up, I just wanted to tell you I love you.' 'I love you, too, Daddy.'

"Now, I ask you, Dan, how many people can say they feel that they've got someone who loves them? I consider myself very fortunate. I mean, do you actually know a self-made man or woman, someone who actually made themselves? No such person exists. It's just impossible. This independence stuff is nothin' but a downright myth. Fabricated. Made up. A lie. Makes me angry, I tell you. I may come across like a tiger, but underneath I'm a real pussy cat."

She reaches for her cup of coffee. Both hands hold the cup as it rests on the crown of her stomach. She pauses and then takes another sip.

"What's happened in Evanston is that we're forgetting the people part of the American Dream. Folks are puttin' all their efforts into acquiring material possessions. Parents have to spend most of their time working. That's nothing new. We've always had to do that. It's when we're working to buy that third and fourth TV set that we're lettin' all this materialism get in the way of our family relationships. Now, I know people have rents and mortgages to pay. I got bills, too, like everyone else. I'm just saying we got to take a good look at what we're doing and not doing.

"What we're forgetting is that somewhere there's

supposed to be another side of this here American Dream. You know, that part that's about good strong moral values, the spiritual side. We've bought into the wrong side of the dream. And I'll tell you something else. If black people don't stop this, we're gonna do ourselves in. Then we'll really let America destroy us.

"We've fought hard for what we've gained since slavery. Evanston isn't Cabrini Green, you know. Family has always been our source of strength. Ask anyone. I guess church, too. But I fear we're losing that strength. We think we don't have the problems they've got in Chicago, or even down South. But we're only foolin' ourselves. If our children are in trouble in school, with the law, getting into gangs, getting into drugs, and getting pregnant, we've got a serious problem, for us and the next generation of black people in Evanston.

"If these problems continue, our children won't be in any kind of condition to inherit whatever we can pass on to them. We can't be paintin' over these problems. We've got to strip 'em down to the bare truth. Like the wood on these walls.

"What's going to be the best for our children? That's the question we've got to ask ourselves. Like I said, parents got to work hard to make a living. Mortgages and rents in Evanston are anything but cheap. I know that. But somewhere we've got to decide which part of the American Dream is gonna help these kids most: the material or the spiritual. It's a tough world, but God knows these kids are looking for attention and direction. I sure was when I was comin' up."

Pauline folds her hands, resting them on her stomach.

"My childhood had it's own ways. I never was in want for anything. I had everything I ever wanted. I always had enough food, I always had enough clean clothes. I had lots of attention from my whole family. Sometimes I think they was too good to me.

"See, I was the first grandchild. Everybody's baby. We lived in the projects then. In those days we was proud to live there, it didn't have the bad connotations it does today. The projects were built for veterans of World War II. My grandfather was a vet and we were proud of him. Now, my family is very achievement-oriented. Everyone is something. My grandfather ran a good business as a barber. My aunt is a supervisor at a key-punch operation. My father worked for the city. So does my uncle. I have a cousin who's in computers, I have another cousin who runs a community job program. If you don't make something of yourself, my family practically closes the book on you."

For a moment, Pauline hesitates at the threshold of her next thought.

"No one can say my Daddy didn't love me. I knew he was proud I was his daughter. But in those days one thing he never did was to take me by the hand and say, 'Pauline, you know, you are my darling daughter and I love you.' He could never say that to me."

She sighs.

"Then why did I get myself pregnant at thirteen? I didn't intend to consciously, but as I think back on it, I must have wanted to unconsciously. It's strange, though. My mother was real open with me. She'd talk to me about anything and everything. She'd talk to me about sex. She'd take me to the library and show me books about a woman's reproductive system, about how women have babies, and how you can protect yourself from getting pregnant. She was real open and caring with me. But I wasn't with her. Or myself. I tuned her out.

"I remember when she told me and my brother how babies were born. I was nine and he was seven. We'd been hearing all kinds of things from kids about the stork and all that, but that never made much sense to me. So one night we asked our mother to tell us. She had a party that night but she could tell we really wanted to know. So she sat us down in the bathroom. I remember she sat on the toilet seat and me and my brother sat on the edge of the tub. She told us about the man's penis and the woman's vagina. The whole bit. Real detailed. I caught on, but my poor brother just looked as bewildered as could be. She asked him, 'You understand?' He said with his big ol' innocent eyes wide open, 'No, Mama.' She tried again but he still didn't catch on. She finally said, 'You know what "Play the Pussy" is?' Oh Lord, did that child's eyes look frightened. He was so upset. He knew what that was all right. He cried and cried. He just couldn't believe his mother did that. He knew other people did that, but not *his* mother. He told everyone his mother played 'Play the Pussy.' He wouldn't talk to her for weeks!"

Pauline and I both laugh.

"But when I got pregnant I was thrown out of junior high. My family decided that if I wanted, I could keep the baby and they'd help me. I got a tutor. If I didn't want the baby an aunt in Chicago, who had lost her baby, was going to adopt mine. I wanted the baby. I told my family that the baby was mine. It was my Picasso. No one could make that baby just the way I did. Not my father, not my mother, not my brothers and sisters. *I* made that baby and it was an expression of *me*.

"That's what I thought then," she says, raising an eyebrow. "But I can say now that I was only a little girl rebelling against her family and having a baby. My boyfriend was the exact opposite of my father and grandfather. His whole family was on welfare. But you couldn't have told me that then.

"Six weeks after my baby was born, me and my boyfriend decided we were going to set up house together. So, in a stolen car we drove to Mississippi with two other boys. I picked up the baby at the baby-sitter's 'n took off without tellin' nobody nothin'. We stayed in an abandoned house down there. We were there over two weeks before my family or anyone found us. It was actually pretty nice. My boyfriend and the others would go out each day and steal whatever we needed. We furnished the whole house out of stolen goods. Pots, pans, chairs, everything. I remember this blue fur chair they got. Even a refrigerator. However, the third time they went back to the same store they were busted. And so was I. I had to spend a couple of nights in jail with my baby. My boyfriend stayed in jail for three years. I went home, but I'd write him nine- and ten-page letters each day. My mother even paid for me to fly down to visit him. Meanwhile, I went back to school. I did pretty well until the second semester of tenth grade. After that, I quit."

She turns toward me. "Yeah, I worry about young girls who seem to think they know everything. I only know better now 'cause I lived through it. I didn't know a thing about mothering. Sure didn't learn about it in school. I had learned all about how you have kids, how you don't have kids, but not one thing about what you do once you have one. Newborns are amazing. They learn so much so fast. When I was a young mother, I didn't even know babies had feelings. I didn't know that the way a mother feels about herself will affect how a baby will grow up emotionally. There was so much I didn't know. When I was a young teenager, I was the only Pauline in the world."

She smiles.

"Take my present junior Partner, Jeanne Hutton. There's a lot that girl's got to learn. About babies and about herself. But she'll make it. She knows I'm talking with her mother. I like to talk with the mothers of all my girls. Jeanne trusts me talking to her mother. One day she might not think it's such a bad thing to do herself.

"Now don't get this picture of me always doin' things for other people. I need time for just myself, too. Friday nights is my time for me. I get into bed 'n turn off the phone. I tell my boys that this is my time out. They understand. Even my little one, the five-year-old. But sometimes he'll come by the room just to check in on me to make sure I'm all right. That's his way of saying he understands but he still wants to be with me. So I have him come and rest with me."

Sitting quietly, Pauline smiles again.

"Before we were married, back when we met in night school, I nearly ran my husband away from me. At the time I just couldn't believe he liked me, me a no-good, teenage mother. I remember asking my mother what was the matter with this man. He opened doors for me and lit my cigarettes practically before I could put the damn things in my mouth. My mother would laugh.

She'd say that's how a gentleman was supposed to act. Well, that nearly blew me away. One night I told Eliot I was scared. He said, 'Scared of what?' I said, 'Scared you'll leave me.' 'Well,' he answered, 'I'm still here, ain't I? Let's get married.' And we were three or four days later. I was seventeen. I've always gotten a lot of support from him.

"We had us a baby soon afterwards. Then I went back to work. I had quit night school. I was in a work-incentive program run by the city. That's where I met Mary, who sort of acted like my senior Partner. She was my supervisor on the job. What a warm and wonderful person she is, Dan. If you ever need to feel good about yourself, just let this woman talk to you. She could make me feel high on myself. At first I thought she was some nosey white woman trying to meddle in my business. But she'd shake her finger at me and tell me not to feel sorry for myself 'cause I was a teen parent. And she was right. I was getting from her something I really needed at the time. My family gave me a lot of love and attention. But they're supposed to do that for you." She nods. "But this white lady sure thought I was someone special. She made me begin to believe in myself. Mary would talk to me for hours. At work. At her home. On the phone. She got me to get my GED. I owe so much to her."

On the coffee table is a photograph of her three boys. She hands it to me.

"I can see a little of myself in each one of my children. My oldest is just like me at thirteen. My middle one I had when I was sixteen, and sure enough if he isn't as easy going and carefree as I was then. He lives as if he doesn't have a care in the world. My baby is just like I

am now, speaking up, outgoing, questioning everything. Lord, that child has a mouth on him! When his
father or I start hollerin' crazy for no good reason, he'll
say, 'I don't like your attitude.'

"My oldest, David, has had to grow up with some
problems. He was my first, back when I didn't know a
thing about myself or about babies. It's not easy to
admit that. He grew up prob'ly feeling bad about himself, the way I felt about myself when he was a small
child. For years I've known he's had some problems,
but I kept denying it. The school officials said he was
just slow. But that wasn't it. He's very quick in the
mind. He just sees things differently. Even strangely
sometimes. But he's not slow.

"About a month ago I had to make the hardest
decision of my life. I sent David to a special residential
school about forty miles from here. My whole family
was against the idea. My grandfather even said he'd
come and take David if I was going to send him away.
He said he wasn't going to give up on David, even if I
was. It wasn't easy for me. But I had to think of what
was going to be best for David. It's no easy thing to tell
yourself your son has some problems because of how he
grew up. When I was younger, I thought I was the
greatest teen mother in the world. I'd take him everywhere I went. And I mean everywhere. But just 'cause
he was with me didn't mean he was getting what he
needed from me. It's a good school he's at. He's getting
the kind of structure and attention I just wasn't able to
give him, especially when he was young.

She looks toward the window.

"I pray for my children and my family every night. I
pray for all these children. But not at any church. I'm

not church-religious. But I do pray. My church is right here at 2037 Jefferson Street.

"I truly believe, Dan, that if I put my mind to something I can do it. Prayer helps give me that strength. I believe the conditions of everyday life can improve. If I can share what I know with the children, with the young girls who are pregnant or who are already mothers, I know I'll have done a lot.

"You see," she says softly, "I almost didn't make it this far. I almost didn't make it to the point where I'd be doing the things I do and saying the things I say. That poem I told you, I wrote that just before I tried suicide. I was fifteen and I wanted to die. I never want to feel as bad as I did then.

"I had taken a bottle of aspirin and sat in a chair. My baby was in his crib next to me. I took the whole bottle. I remember he had on a light brown-beige shirt and gray pants. As I was fading away I could hear him call out, 'Mommy! Mommy!' I guess my grandmother heard him and came in. I didn't come to until I was in the hospital.

"I was in psychiatric care for two weeks. For six months after that I saw a doctor. He was a wonderful, caring, and sensitive man. He gave me the kind of support I really needed then. He listened to me and he helped me understand a lot of what I was feeling. I learned a very important thing as a result of that experience. I know how lonely and desperate a person can feel. I felt so bad trying to grow up and be a mother at the same time. It's not easy, even with your family being there for you. So I try to care for others, particularly teenage mothers, as that doctor and Mary cared for me. I used to feel guilty because sometimes I didn't want anything to do with my child. I'll never forget the doctor saying that was normal! He said he'd really be worried about me if I never had a thought like that.

"I know other mothers have the same feelings and someone's got to tell them what that doctor told me. That man saved my life.

"Somewhere some girl might end up dead like I almost did. And if I can help prevent that I will. Maybe that's why I try to do good things for people. Maybe it's my need to be needed. Maybe it's also that I'm scared I'll be left alone."

Pauline stares at a paint scraper. "You know what they say, 'if you give, you'll receive, and what goes around comes around.' "

Movin' On

I

I recall my first day at Our Place. I am driving north to Evanston from Chicago feeling both nervous and excited about my new job. I roll down the car windows. A hot August wind helps ease the mid-morning humidity.

My assignment is to gain some sense of what the teens think and how they feel about the center. I am also to get to know some of the teen mothers and get them to talk about their lives as adolescent parents. Assuming all works out as planned, I am to write a series of life studies to convey something of the quality of their young lives.

All along Ridge Road I wonder about the project. How am I to get these kids to talk to me? Will they feel comfortable with me? Will I feel comfortable talking and listening to them? Will I end up staring at their bulging stomachs?

I fear I will stick out like a sore thumb. "Oh, no," I think, "how phallic an image can there be?" At least my unconscious knows I am about to enter a world of teenagers and sex and babies.

I park the car. I take a deep breath. I walk through

the front door. I am acutely aware of them watching me. Here I am. I am white, they are black. I am male, most of them are female. I am in my mid-twenties, they are all teenagers. I am Jewish, and most of them must be Christian.

I notice that these observations don't include the category of parenthood. Hmm . . . ? I am not a parent and they are all parents, or will be very soon.

I take a few more steps inside the door. "Why not," I say to myself, "we've got a lot in common."

I approach a table of young mothers who are playing cards. A large girl with a lofty Afro stands before me with a baby in her outstretched arms. "Would you like to hold my baby?" she asks.

"Why sure," I answer. I am stunned. This is great, I haven't been in the place for more than thirty seconds and one of these mothers talks to me. More than that, she asks me to hold her baby.

For several minutes I hold her year-old daughter, standing in the same place where she was handed to me. We make funny noises at each other. She laughs. Several more minutes go by. My new-found ease begins to erode. I try to watch the card game. I keep scanning the hall for the mother of the child in my arms.

"She does that all the time," one of the card players eventually says to me without taking her eyes off her cards. "She does that to anyone, boy, 'n I guess you're it today."

They all laugh.

"I guess so, but do you know where she might be?"

"Your guess is as good as mine. Don't worry, she'll be back. She don't usually leave the person stranded *all* day!"

I continue to play with the baby, as much for my sake as for hers.

"Hold on, mister," I am informed by the girl who has been speaking to me, "I'll see if I can find her for you. She's not supposed to do that, anyhow."

A few minutes later, the girl returns with the mother of my warm and playful little prop. "Isn't she pretty?" the mother comments as though she had been standing there with us all this time. "Oh, now, look at those big brown eyes," she coos. "Some of the other mothers call her 'Chocolate Eyes.' Ain't they somethin'?" The mother is smiling and her daughter smiles back. "But, girl, what did you do to your dress? Gettin' it all dirty! I told you not to go crawlin' on this dirty hall floor. You should be in the child-care room. Did you let her play on the floor?" she asks me as she brushes off her daughter's white dress.

"No, I just held her, just the way you gave her to me."

"Good. I mean, I'm not sayin' you did or nothin', but it's just not good for her to play in the hallway." She pauses. "You sure you don't want to keep her for a while more?"

"I've got to find a guy named Ed Harrod. Is he here? Maybe I can play with her later. How's that?"

"You *sure* you don't want to now?" she asks.

"I'll find you when I'm finished talking with Ed. I have to let him know I'm here."

II

That's how I met Joanne Johnson and her daughter, Renee. They were the first people I met at Our Place. At sixteen, Joanne has been a mother for just over a year. She was one of the first girls to use Our Place. "A Founding Mother," she will say. Joanne wants to return to high school, but she feels the difficulties of her first year of parenthood haven't given her the time she would need. Since she isn't working, she often spends much of her time at Our Place. Like all teens, she uses the center to meet her immediate needs. If there is something better to do, she'll do that instead.

Joanne has a particular way of using the center. She will participate intensively in a host of activities for a period of two or three weeks and then will not return to the center for another two or three weeks. Sometimes we won't see her for several months. During these periods, she'll make a phone call now and again to Mrs. Henry, one of the staff. Joanne will check in to ask how everybody is doing and to let us know how she is doing, too. But each time she comes back. And when she returns, she reenters the life of the center as though she has never left.

My friendship with Joanne and Renee has developed over our many lunches together. Joanne likes one restaurant in particular. Good burgers and good fries. It has wide booths, too; wide enough for Renee's baby chair.

One afternoon in early spring, we meet at Our Place before going to lunch. We've developed an unspoken routine for these outings. Joanne will put on Renee's snowsuit, boots, hat, and mittens and then hand Renee to me while she puts on her own coat. Usually, Joanne wants me to take Renee to the car. Once Joanne is seated, I'll return Renee to her and then walk around to the driver's seat. Renee likes playing with the switch for the windshield wipers. Her mother will grab her hand

to pull it away, but only after Renee has already suc-
ceeded in making the wipers flash by our eyes. Renee is
quick. She'll giggle and smile with pride at her great
achievement. It's all part of our routine. Once at the
restaurant, Joanne will hand me her daughter to carry
inside. Joanne likes having me do that; she says she
likes having a man around.

Mother and daughter sit together. I sit across from
them next to the pile of coats. Renee is a grabber; she
loves to get her hands on anything within reach. Whatever the object, she'll bang it, tear it, suck on it, anything. Her mother knows this only too well. Experience
has taught Joanne to keep the knives and forks out of
Renee's reach. She moves the glass of water, too. The
napkin Renee can keep; it doesn't make any noise.
But, even the napkin has its hazards. Eventually, Joanne has to fish out its torn pieces from Renee's mouth.
Renee's initial grimace turns to a smile as she searches
for something else to grab and explore.

Joanne orders for Renee first and then for herself.
Negotiating the terrain of a conversation over lunch
with an energetic eighteen-month-old at the table is no
easy matter.

"I wish I was married, Dan," Joanne says as she
keeps one arm across Renee's lap. "I really wish I
was."

"Got anyone special in mind?" I ask.

"Not really, not yet at any rate. I just wish I was
married." She reaches for a glass of water. "You interested? How 'bout you and me?"

"Not now, thanks."

"I think I'd be a good wife. That's really all I want in
life—a little family: me and Renee and my man. Who-

ever he may turn out to be." She rolls her eyes. "Bein' a housewife is what I want to be. I like workin' around the house and makin' things look good and keepin' the place clean. I'm not the kind who wants to go out and go to work everyday. I want me a man who'll support me and who wants a good woman at home." She looks over at Renee. "And he's got to be a good father, too."

Renee begins to squirm in her seat. "Sit still, girl," Joanne orders. She reaches in her purse and gives Renee a bottle filled with milk. Renee puts her mouth around its nipple, holding the bottle in both hands. Then, like a trumpet player, she tilts its bottom in the air and sucks quietly.

"Marriage is real important to me," Joanne goes on to say, "it means your life is more secure, more stable, you know. You have a house, a permanent home where you got all your things together, in one place. I think I'll be married by the time I finish high school, but who knows, maybe even sooner. But no more kids, that's for sure. At least not for now. I want to be married first for a while before I have me any more children, and even then I'll have only one more. Two's plenty for me. I've got Renee. My next one, I hope will be a boy. Fathers like to have boys, 'specially if they've got a girl already. Yeah, a boy and a girl. That'd be nice. But no more 'n that, 'specially not now. I learned my lesson."

"What do you mean lesson?"

" 'Bout havin' babies while I was so young. You see, lookin' back on things I would have done things a lot different; I'd prob'ly still be a virgin today." She blushes. "I'd a been a virgin till I got married. But what can I do? Can't change that fact, right? Or this one," she says as she wipes the corners of Renee's mouth.

The waitress brings our food. Joanne cuts Renee's hot dog into small pieces. Then she puts a little ketchup and a bit of mustard on her hamburger.

"It's hard bein' a parent, 'specially all by yourself. Don't let anyone fool you," she says as she chews a french fry. "And it would've been a lot harder at times if it wasn't for Pauline. She's my Partner, y'know. She'd tell me how things was for her when she was my age and bein' a mother 'n all. She's a smart lady. She shows me how to do all kinds of stuff. I guess she's been sort of a mother to me since I ain't had one since I was four. I didn't have no mother to tell me stuff 'bout babies; how you take care of 'em, 'n feed 'em, 'n clothe 'em. Pauline showed me a lot of that. And my older sisters did, too."

Joanne takes another bite from her hamburger. Renee chews a piece of her hot dog and then takes it out of her mouth. Ketchup is smeared on her left cheek. She begins to squirm again.

"Do you think you've become better at being a mother than you first thought you were?" I ask.

"No," she says with a laugh, as she turns toward her daughter. "Now eat your hot dog, child, and quit causin' trouble. She can't sit still, Dan. She's like that all the time. She's a handful for me. Bein' a parent is a lot of responsibility and I don't think I was really ready for it. But, you know, I do the best I can. Pauline's been a big help to me. She's even showed me some stuff 'bout cookin'. But I haven't used Partners as good as I should've. Been too busy; just too busy movin' all the time. Do you realize I've lived in seven different places since Renee was born. None of these places work out too well for me. I just moved to this basement room a lady was renting out. I've been in a couple of places like that before. It's not too bad, but I know I won't be there long. I started out at my father's, but when I got pregnant I had to find me a place of my own. My stepmother had him make me go. He didn't really want to, but I wanted to anyways. I've been movin' ever since. He helps me move, though, and he give me rent money, too."

Renee bangs her plate on the table. Joanne puts her hand on the plate, keeping it down. Renee does it again. This time Joanne pushes the plate toward me, out of Renee's grasp. Renee begins to cry. Joanne gives Renee her bottle.

"You know, I knew all about birth control. Knew how to use it, where to get it. Everything. Just didn't want to."

"That simple?"

"Yeah. Me and this white girl I used to run with got pregnant at the exact same time. All along we kept sayin' we should go down to the clinic and get the birth control pills. But we just never got around to it. I guess we just didn't want to use it. You know what they say, if you want to bad enough. . . . But we just didn't. You see, I didn't want to bother with no birth control when I wanted to have sex . . . ugh . . . I hate that word . . . when I wanted to make love, I mean. You know, with someone special, who you care about. I love to make love and when I want to have it, I don't want to be fussin' with no birth control."

"But with birth control pills, you just take them on a regular basis so you won't have to fuss at the last minute," I explain.

"Yeah, but with the pill, it means your plannin'

straight out to do it with somebody, like you're in-tendin' to. It makes you feel bad, like you've been thinkin' 'bout doin' it all during the day. I just don't like birth control. It's either a big fuss or it makes you feel sorta bad, like guilty kinda."

Renee kicks the bottom of the table. Everything jumps. She stops after she sees the look her mother gives her.

"I got pregnant first when I was fifteen. I knew somethin' was up when I started noticin' I was missin' my periods. But I didn't tell anyone."

"How come?"

" 'Cause if I had, my father woulda made me get an abortion, and I wanted a baby. But after I missed my second period I started gettin' scared. So one night while my father's watchin' TV, I sorta walked over to him 'n said, 'Hey, Dad, what would you do if I ever got pregnant?' He said, 'What?' And I said it again. And he said, 'Why, girl! Look at her face, she's smilin'! Oh, girl you ain't pregnant, are you? You know I can't afford no other child!'

"So I decided to have an abortion. So did my friend, the white girl. That abortion was awful. It really made me feel bad. The doctor there was antagonizin' me, askin' me, 'Why did you get pregnant? You know you're not old enough.' He really upset me with his dumb ol' questions. Really. You know I had my abortion on my birthday . . . December 27. I guess it was my birthday present to my father."

She laughs. "What did you get for your birthday? An abortion."

Renee has finished her bottle and is restless again.

The waitress comes by and winks at Renee as she clears the table. Joanne smiles at the waitress but tries to ignore Renee's fidgeting.

"By the next month, though, I was pregnant again. I just really wanted a baby, one of my very own. A few nights after my abortion I was with some friends and we was all in couples. We started kissin' 'n stuff 'n were feelin' sorta uncomfortable, if you know what I mean. So we kept on kissin' and, y'know, how one thing leads into another.

"Now don't get me wrong, now, we didn't make love, me and this guy, right away. No, not me. I'm not like that, not like that at all. My reputation matters to me. I've got to feel comfortable with someone and that means I got to know the person for a while. It didn't take long for me to want to do it with him. But I waited about a month.

"So on that night we made love, like I was sayin'. Now, Arnell, he's different than me. He's about twenty-seven 'n he wanted to have sex with me right there on our first date, but that's how most men are."

Joanne takes a napkin and soaks it in a glass of water before wiping off Renee's face and hands. "My baby here was intentional, all right. I wanted her so bad I just kept my mouth quiet and didn't tell nobody nothin'. Not even about my morning sickness. It didn't become public knowledge till I was six months gone. And by then I couldn't hide much. I was determined to have a baby. I really liked Arnell. I suppose by gettin' pregnant I thought I could keep him, that he'd stay with me."

"Did he?"

"No. After I got pregnant he and his family wouldn't have nothin' to do with me or the baby. He just denied everything.

"And when I did announce my pregnancy I think it broke up my father's second marriage, too. His wife just couldn't accept me. But they was havin' troubles anyways. That's why I went to stay with my brother before I got my own place."

Joanne pauses as she wipes a smudge off the table.

"When I was in the delivery room havin' Renee, I was thinkin' what I was gonna name my baby. I was really hopin' for a boy. But when I saw that baby's head come out, you know, as I was lookin' up into that big mirror they have for you, I stopped watchin' and just kept concentratin' on havin' the baby. And, boy, was I screamin'! I had my cousin there with me and she said she almost went deaf. I was screamin' everybody's name. I remember I kept callin', 'Mama! Mama!' Pretty weird, me callin' for my Mama when she's been dead all these years."

Joanne sits quietly. "My father says it's a good thing I have that baby. He loves it and he thinks it's the best lookin' baby he's ever seen. My stepmother, she can't deal, no how. She can't deal with me 'cause she hasn't had no kids of her own.

"But you know, after Renee was born; I mean like the very day after she was born, the whole thrill was gone. I went home and felt like cryin'. All of a sudden it hit me: I'm a mother. And I had this little baby to take care of. I guess it's been all right, but it ain't been easy, it ain't been what I thought it would be. I just like the way little babies look. They're so small 'n cute. I really wanted one. I just didn't realize how much they need you. I mean you really got to take care of 'em 'cause they can't take care of themselves. I guess that's what I meant when I said I've learned my lesson. Thinkin' 'bout havin' a baby 'n even bein' pregnant with one is a whole lot different than actually havin' one twenty-four hours a day, havin' to feed it, get up when it does in the middle of the night 'n change its diapers. And there's no relief for me. I'm the only one around to do it; at least mostly, that is. That's a reason why I want to be married. A husband could really help out a lot."

Joanne turns to Renee who has climbed out of her seat and stands looking over at the people in the booth behind her. They are playing with her. "Come on around here, Renee," Joanne says, "Dan and I ain't ready to leave yet.

"Can I ask you a question, Dan?" Joanne asks without looking at me. "It's sort of personal."

"That's all right, go ahead."

"You sure?"

"I'm sure."

She hesitates. She still isn't looking at me.

"Are you a virgin?"

"No. Why?"

"I don't know; you sound like it."

"Oh yeah?" I wonder with surprise.

"All the other men I know are always, you know, trying to rap to me, trying to get into somethin' funky with me. And you don't."

She picks up Renee and places her on her lap. "I hope I find a good man someday; 'n someday soon at that."

III

"I don't like dresses," Joanne says to me angrily. "Some people tell me my legs are too fat, others whistle at me 'n hassle me 'cause they like my legs. That's why I like to wear pants and pants suits. No hassles one way or the other. Besides, I don't got a nice dress anyways."

We speak on a hot June afternoon in the living room of the small apartment she recently has rented. Still in her bathrobe, Joanne is surprised by my unannounced visit. I have come to give her tickets for the special celebration to be held that evening to honor all the young mothers in the Partners Program. Joanne has not been at Our Place in almost two months. She has forgotten all about the elaborate plans for the evening. As we talk, Renee plays quietly in a corner.

"I don't know, Dan, I feel real funny about going and not having a nice dress. I wish I'da planned ahead more."

"You can always wear one of your nice pants suits," I offer.

"Naw, not for tonight. Tonight I gotta look nice, real nice. Like a lady. I gotta have a nice dress; otherwise I just can't go."

She pauses.

"Oh, I'm so nervous. What time does it start?"

"Seven o'clock."

"What time is it now?"

"Two-thirty."

"Oh, what am I gonna do?" she moans.

"Have you talked to Pauline lately?"

"Yeah. I don't know why this slipped my mind. Maybe she's got something for me."

I drive Joanne and Renee the few blocks to Pauline's

house. Pauline says they'll find something "real pretty" for Joanne.

For a month, the girls at Our Place have been busy making dresses and making decisions for this big night. It is their night; they are "movin' on." Twenty-one young mothers have decided, along with their fifteen senior Partners, that they are ready to move on in their lives. After a year of close friendship, the girls feel they are now ready to have their older women friends lend that support to a newer and younger group of teen mothers.

A public celebration is suggested. A special event to mark this special moment. Even the name of the celebration had to reflect its special qualities. Graduations happen in school. Confirmations happen in church. "A Progressional Ceremony," offers an adult mother. A teen mother counters. "How 'bout just callin' it 'Movin' On,' 'cause that's what we're doin', ain't it?"

The girls will not be "movin' on," from Our Place; they have made sure of that. A new place is created for them and by them. Making dresses and making decisions: "Movin' On" is to toast their transition from "Partners" to "Sisterhood." In Sisterhood they will learn to offer each other the kind of friendship they have been receiving from their senior Partners.

The girls intend this celebration to be special, to be different. And by its very nature it has to be different. Our Place has rented a large hall at the Holiday Inn to host this celebration for twenty-one teenage mothers. The Holiday Inn. It has to be special.

The sparkle of the hotel's lobby, the hushed sounds

of footsteps on hallway carpets, the high loft of the ceilings add an extra edge to the excitement of last-minute arrangements. Everyone looks sharp. Friends, family, and staff; over one hundred and twenty people sit at the many tables that fill the hall. Long banquet tables run along the back wall. Three teen fathers shoot me a wink and tell me they have come for the food. To their right sits the disc jockey and his tower of records. The rhythms of festive talk and social movement play counterpoint to the DJ's latest selection.

By seven-thirty most people have arrived. Someone dims the lights. A restless anticipation can be heard. I stand by the door waiting anxiously to let Joanne in; she is late. Delores Holmes, director of Our Place, approaches the podium. I feel the doorknob turn. It is Joanne in a lovely maroon dress.

A spotlight hits Mrs. Holmes. She welcomes all who came. Bernice Weissbourd, president of Family Focus, says a few words, too. Ruth Vaughn, a member of the auxiliary board, is also introduced. These strong women set the pace. Spirits are high.

Entertainment follows. A young woman in a light summer dress sings Gershwin's "Summertime" and then recites a poem she has recently written. Another young woman performs a modern dance she has choreographed to Johnny Mathis's recording of "You Light Up My Life." Then an all-male choir sings three gospel songs, and a dramatic reading of Nikki Giovanni's poem "Children" is followed by Vachel Lindsay's "The Congo." A teen mother new to Our Place shares a poem she has written for the occasion.

Then, Davene Dolan, spokeswoman for the senior

Partners, walks toward the podium. That's the girls' cue to line up alphabetically at the back of the hall. The processional will soon begin.

"Partners," Davene begins, "this is indeed a special night for *all* of us."

"Hmm hmm!" someone calls out.

"In a sense, we older Partners are movin' on, too. After all, you were our first Partners, and we'll be movin' on to our new ones.

"It's so good to see so many of you here. As your Partners we hope to have given you inspiration and support, letting you know that we care and that you're not alone. We would like to leave you with these thoughts.

"Believe in yourself as we believe in you. Love yourself as we care for you. The time will come when you say, I have made it, I see the day. We believe in all of you and know that you will carry on because you and your children are our future. We hope we have given you strengths and aims in life. Ain't no stopping you now," she said as she raises her voice. "You're on the move!"

Through the roar of applause I hear one girl shout, "Then let's get movin'!" The girls stand poised but they stand restlessly, too. Joanne whispers something to Shirley Jarvis, the card player I met on my first day at Our Place.

One by one, as Davene calls out their names, each girl walks down the center aisle.

"Caroline Booth: she's a new mother and plans to continue her education in computer programming. She's a graduate of Evanston Township High School.

"Valerie Curtis: she's the mother of her handsome ten-month-old son, Jerome. She's movin' on to Sisterhood!

"Patricia Davis: she passed her GED last month and is busy preparing herself for a new baby . . . which looks like it ought to be comin' any minute now!"

Each girl receives a Certificate of Progression from Bernice Weissbourd. Pauline Thompson gives each girl a rose and a kiss.

Katharine Franklin.

Jewel Hillman.

Ruby Lee Holiday.

Rose after rose, each girl takes her place next to her companions; not in a straight line but in the gentle bow of a semicircle.

Cynthia Isaacs.

Elizabeth James.

Shirley Jarvis.

More certificates and more roses.

"Joanne Johnson," Davene says. "With her beautiful daughter, Renee, Joanne is definitely movin' on!" Joanne tries to hide how she feels. She blushes as she walks. She doesn't know Bernice so she accepts her certificate hurriedly. Pauline kisses her and then gives Joanne her rose.

With each rose, the curve of the circle expands.

Monique Tilden.

Sandra Turner.

Diane Wright.

The semicircle is now complete. Quiet music plays. Cynthia Booth hands each girl a candle. She lights her own and then lights Valerie's with its flame. Valerie then lights Patricia's; and so on until Sandra lights

Diane's. Without sound, Cynthia and Diane bring the group to a full circle. They hold out their arms; a white candle in their left hands, a red rose in their right.

Suddenly, the chorus of voices chants, *"We're Movin' on!"* The music grows louder as they chant, *"We're Movin' on!"* one more time.

It is several minutes before the cheering and hugging subsides and the crowd turns its attention to Katharine Franklin at the podium.

"Hi, everyone," Katharine begins. "I'm scared! My fellow Partners gave me four weeks to write a speech for this occasion and I haven't got a thing to say."

Her first line pulls in a big laugh.

"Naw, just kidding," she continues. In two lines she has won her audience.

"I'm really glad to be here. By here, I mean a part of this program, Partners. Now I know some of you are saying, Partners, what's Partners? Partners is a group started by Family Focus, Our Place, in the summer of 1980 with the intention of helping young single mothers and mothers-to-be. To help them, I mean us, mentally and spiritually, each teen Partner, was given an adult Partner who at one time or another was rocking the same boat. So they knew just how it felt to be a young, unwed mother or mother-to-be. Their purpose was to be a guide, someone to go to when we needed advice, help or just someone to talk to, go places and do things with.

"By and by, we grew. Then new and younger girls started coming into the group and the girls already in the group were getting older and at least some of us were gettin' wiser. Our needs were changing by age and state of mind. So we realized that we now had to help two fairly different groups—the older ones and the younger ones. It was time for the older ones to move on and the younger ones to move in.

"But we didn't want to lose the ones we had. That's when we decided on taking another step; to give the younger teen parents the benefits of the program by gaining the wisdom, courage, and strength the adult Partners have to offer without letting us older teen Partners go.

"In the time that I've been in Partners, I've gained a lot, even more than I can handle. But I am indeed grateful for what I have been able to achieve and receive. You can ask anyone. I've come a long way. I've come from being a tough little kid nicknamed, Cookie, to me, Katharine, even though now and then I'm still called Cookie for fun.

"But I'm not by myself. I have a handsome two-year-old son and a wonderful Partner who I can say has been there everytime I needed her with a strong hand . . . and a soft heart. And then there's Mrs. Holmes, who believes in nothing but giving, and Mrs. Henry and Mrs. Richmond, who truly believe in the way to reach someone is through their stomachs! And our Nurse Todd, who knows all the real medical terms. . . . "

Katharine has to pause to let the laughter quiet down.

"And to the rest of the wonderful staff of Our Place and to our adult Partners, we, the younger Partners, say, 'Thanks for bein' there.' " She blows a kiss to her audience, just the way she has indicated on the last page of her prepared speech: "(blow a kiss!)"

Mrs. Holmes puts her arm around Katharine as they

face a standing ovation. Katharine begins to laugh.
Mrs. Holmes steps up to the microphone.

"I just want to say something to you all. Especially to
you senior Partners. Not too many people are willing
to work with teens these days. And dreams are only
dreams without the willing and active people to help
our young people through the very real and potential
troubles that can come their way. You know how much
I love you. . . . "

"We love you, too, Delores!" an old friend shouts.

"You've gone a long way with me and the rest of the
staff. I wish I had a million dollars to give you all. . . . "

"I wish you did, too!" jibes a senior Partner.

"I think this night just goes to show what some of us
have always known; kids will act in a fashion similar to
the way they are treated by adults. If you treat them as
just a bunch of crazy, worthless teens, they'll act the
part. But, they'll rise to the occasion if they're shown
that they are worthy and important.

"You are all wonderful. Now, let's get something to
eat and start dancing!"

The DJ hears his cue and goes to work. Instantly a
few teens hit the dance floor. Several senior Partners
begin serving food at the long banquet table. The three
teen fathers who had shot me a wink are first in line.
Some teens show their certificates and roses to friends
and family. Everywhere people are talking.

But near me, at a table in the corner, Joanne and
Pauline are crying. Although seated, they hug each
other for several minutes.

"Oh, Pauline, oh, Pauline. It was so nice," Joanne
manages to say through her tears. "I felt like I was

important to people, with everyone telling me now nice I look and all. They was real happy to see me. I really felt it. Like they cared 'bout me. Aside from the day Renee was born, this is the happiest night of my life. I just really felt wanted, like I was part of one big family."

IV

Within two weeks, Joanne has moved again, this time to the west side of Chicago. Although I've heard she has stopped by Our Place once or twice and calls Mrs. Henry on occasion, I have neither seen nor heard from Joanne in over eight months. A friend told me she had seen Joanne in Grant Park, in downtown Chicago, walking with Renee. Joanne had told my friend that she would soon be married. That was in the autumn.

It drizzles on the March morning I drive to meet Joanne. She is moving yet again, now to Alabama. She had called Our Place the day before and I had answered the phone. She wanted Nurse Todd to send her Renee's medical records and to tell Mrs. Henry she has decided to move south to live with her older brother and his family. She asked me if I would take her out to lunch one last time, but not in the Loop or around the west side of Chicago.

I follow her directions. Chicago. West Madison Street. The Olive Branch Mission. Just ring the door bell, someone will let you in. At eleven o'clock, okay? A little extra sleep will be needed for the long bus trip south.

I see Renee first. She has grown so much. Over two years old now. Joanne has changed, too. Her long hair is now cut short and she has lost some weight. We stand in a large dining hall, dimly lit by a fluorescent glow. Sparse but clean. Two elderly men sit together at a table. An older woman sits by herself. A large blackboard hangs on the far wall.

"Bet you're wonderin' what I'm doin' here," Joanne says to me. "It's pretty different than where I was when I was in Evanston. Right?"

"Looks like it."

"You see, Dan, I'm into the Lord now; you know, the Bible, and not sinning. I found the Lord." She speaks calmly. She seems more settled than I had remembered her. "I'm more open to God now, much more than before when I was a kid. I used to be open to all kinds of the Devil's temptations, like not praying at night. Still am, but I'm workin' on it. The Lord's saved me several times from some mighty mean situations. He gave me this place to stay when I really needed it. I had went to church, you know, as a little girl, like all kids do, but I could never sit still like they wanted me to. I be always talkin' and movin' around and lookin' at the boys.

"But it's different now. I know how important the Word is to me now. It was like I had woke up and knew somethin' I had always known."

"How long have you been here?"

" 'Bout two weeks. I came here from this place I was stayin' at, Good Shepherd."

On our way to lunch we are to stop at Good Shepherd to pick up what remains of Joanne's worldly belongings. Nearly everything, including her Certificate of Progression and her only photograph of her mother, had been stolen from an apartment where she had been staying. Like old times, I carry Renee to the car.

We drive north to Good Shepherd. Around the corner will be Wrigley Field.

"I've been all over, Dan, since you saw me last. I've been down to Florida and Tennessee. I was with my boyfriend down there, but I left him three different times. That's how come I'm going to Alabama. I got to get away and get settled. My brother wanted me to come down. My boyfriend, Calvin, he's been followin' me every time I leave him. In Tennessee, a few weeks ago, we stopped for something to eat. He went to the bathroom and I grabbed Renee and we took off. Two nights ago he shows up at the mission, yellin' at the top of his lungs for me. He's hollerin' for me out there on the street at two o'clock in the morning!"

"That's why you didn't want to have lunch on the West Side?" I ask.

"Yep. I'm afraid he'll be waitin' for me. Things with him were real good at first. We went down to Florida where we were gonna get married. We had us a little house to stay in. Renee would play outside. It was real nice. He had a job pickin' oranges. That was in December. I even tried pickin' oranges once. But I quit after one day. It was too hot. I hated it.

"But then he lost his job. And some time after that he started hittin' me and slappin' me around. And, you know I won't take that from no man. That's when I started leavin' him. He talked a lot of stuff 'bout bein' into the Lord, but I didn't believe him, though I wanted to. That's how I ended up here at Good Shepherd. You know, it's a shelter for battered women."

We pull into the parking lot at Good Shepherd. Joanne goes to get her things. I hold Renee in my lap. She has fallen asleep. Cracker crumbs are on her lips and on her coat. Joanne returns with a large green garbage bag filled with clothes.

The hours move into the afternoon, and after lunch, near the Good Shepherd, we drive to the south end of the Loop where Joanne needs to pick up a pair of shoes she has left at a shoemaker's. We continue to talk about her travels and her plans.

"I'm still sad about not gettin' married," she remarks as she looks out the car window onto Halsted Street. "But I see Calvin's not the right man for me. Down in Florida, I'd be thinkin' of my baby first, and he'd be thinkin' of himself first. I'd cook somethin' for Renee and he'd come along and eat it all for himself. That just ain't right. And he wouldn't take care of his body neither. He'd still be drinkin' and smokin' reefer and then tellin' me how he's tryin' to be into the Lord.

"I really think I know what it means to be a parent now. I've had to take care of Renee and myself all by myself for the last seven months. Calvin was sure no help. Well, at first he was, but that didn't last too long. I know we're better off without him.

"I'm goin' down to Alabama for good, Dan. I might be back in a few years or somethin' to visit everyone in Evanston, but I'm going for good. I was born and raised in Evanston. But I like the warm weather. And besides, I'll be busy. I've decided to go back to high school. I'll be livin' with my brother and his wife, so that'll be good for me and Renee. I got to get on with gettin' my education and my career. Maybe I'll go to college in a couple of years. I'd really like to do that. My brother says there's even a place by the house for a garden. I don't know; I think I'd like to try that, too.

"I'll leave a place on an impulse, Dan. I'll just get up and go. That's what happened in that restaurant in Tennessee. But somehow I don't think I'll be doin' that in 'Bama. I'm really plannin' to stay. The Lord's gotten me this far and has given this chance to me and Renee and I don't plan on wastin' it. That's how I see Our Place and Pauline. The Lord gave me a chance there, too." She smiles. "Besides, I might meet a good man while I'm down there."

I park in front of the Olive Branch Mission. The day's drizzle has turned to mist. Joanne carries her bag of clothes, I carry Renee. In an hour they'll be gone. In twenty-six hours they'll be in Alabama.

I set Renee down by a table near the blackboard in the dining hall but she won't stand up. Each time I try, she lets her knees bend and her legs collapse under her. Joanne approaches me for a hug goodbye. Renee holds her mother's leg. They stand, framed by the edges of the blackboard. No one says anything. I notice something is written on the blackboard behind them. I squint to take a closer look. It is from the Book of Revelations:

For the lamb in the midst of the throne will be their shepherd, and he will guide them to springs of living water; and God will wipe away every tear from their eyes.

Rock Steady

I

Sitting in one of the brown wooden chairs that circle a small table in the parent room, Ed stares out onto the street through a large picture window on his left. Ed has just joined the staff at Our Place, two months after the center opened. "You know what's been bugging me lately?" he says, turning to one of the women staff members seated across from him. "We're spending all our time helping out the teen moms."

The woman looks puzzled. "Isn't that what we're supposed to be doing?"

Ed doesn't have a chance to answer.

"Now I heard that. You've got all kinds of guys wanderin' through here all the time, but there ain't nothin' for us to do here," says Ardis Taylor, who sits on a couch nearby. At sixteen, he speaks with conviction. "Shoot, this place is for chicks. You say this is 'Our Place' . . . for all teen parents . . . well, you know that's a joke. I'm a father, right? And that makes me a parent, right? But this isn't *Our* Place, it's *Her* Place.

"I mean, what about the guys who come by here to see their women, or who want to see their baby? Or how 'bout the guys who come by here just lookin' for somethin' to do?" He stands up and walks toward the door. "I'm serious," he warns, "If you want this place to work, then you got to start doin' somethin' for us teen fathers as well. Dig?"

II

"I remember that day very well," Ed recalls to me one afternoon about a year later. "I remember the whole thing, most definitely." I stand with Ed outside the front door. Every afternoon he takes a broom and sweeps the sidewalk in front of Our Place. It's his daily ritual. "Helps the kids have pride in the place," he will say.

"I identified with that young man right away," Ed says as he sweeps. "I knew he had to feel out of place if I was feelin' it too. Right off the bat I felt uncomfortable, excluded, just like he did. The program wasn't reaching the fathers. People had their hands full with the young ladies. But, like the young man said, it might as well have been called 'Her' Place. The fellas were reaching out to us just by coming here, and there wasn't nothing for them to do. I had a long talk with Ardis about what he thought ought to be done around here and I asked him how he liked the idea of us startin' a fathers' group.

"Most of the fellas was simply driftin' in and out. Some had quit school and only a couple were working at the time. I thought, wow, that'd be a dynamite way to offer the young men some support in trying to create some direction in their lives. They sure were seeking it. And they were serious about it, too. Inside of two or three months, I'd say, we had over eleven regulars comin' every week. Every Wednesday night. Sure it would've been outasight if more had come. And you and I both know there's a lot more than eleven fathers out there," he says, pointing his broom toward the street.

"But the fact that eleven guys cared enough to come to a fathers' rap group at a center for teen parents is very significant. Very significant, indeed. I mean, how many guys can admit that they're fathers, much less talk about it in a group with other fellas their own age? And they talk about all kinds of business; like jobs and wanting to be employed so's they can support their babies. And school, too, or getting their GED or pursuing something in college.

"These fellas ain't afraid to talk about how they're feeling, or how things are goin' with their young ladies, or about what's goin' down at home. It's encouraging to see a group of guys trying to tackle some of the problems they got to deal with. It's almost like they've *got* to talk. These fellas want to learn a lot about life and about growing up. I can see that in their eyes and I can hear it in their questions. And there's a lot they've got to learn, too.

"But I hand it to 'em for trying, 'cause there sure are a lot of their peers who aren't. Sometimes I can be amazed that these street-wise, street-hustling guys want to spend time in a place filled with so many moms and babies. It says something, don't it? There's got to be something special about these young men, 'cause this place ain't no gym and it sure ain't no pool hall."

Ed smiles. "You see that young fella over there?" he says pointing down the block. "That kid is a real gas. I remember him coming in here one Wednesday night and we were talking about responsibility and child care. You couldn't get this cat to look at a diaper, much less change one. As far as he was concerned, and some of the other fellas as well, child rearing was the mother's responsibility. No man diapers babies or pushes strollers in the park. You should have heard him: 'She can change the diapers, she can wash the baby, she can feed the baby, she can take the baby to the doctor's, she can do it all.' He was arguing that as fathers, their job was to make money to pay for the diapers, the doctor, the food, and the clothing.

"Well, well. A picture *is* worth a thousand words, now ain't it," Ed says with a laugh. We watch the young father walk down the street toward the park. He is pushing his daughter in a stroller. Ed shakes his head and says, "Well, I'll be!

"You know, changes like that are tough, man. Teenagers are about as impatient a crowd as you'll find. They get an idea in their head one second and then think it can be done the next. One thing I definitely noticed was the frustration and powerless feeling these fellas suffered from. They were confused, man, like so many teens. And when they got an idea about doin' something, they'd really have no realistic way to go about getting what they want. And not only did some of 'em not know what they wanted, but they didn't even have any idea of how to find out.

"Take this one cat, Ronny, for example. He comes to me sayin' he wants a job, needs it real bad, has to have it right away. So we talk. Right away I can tell he's got no idea of how to look for a job. He's fifteen and he's had no interviewing experience, no knowledge of how to dress for an interview, no understanding of where or how to begin lookin' for one. So I ran a few workshops for the guys where we learned about filling out applications, role-playing, rehearsing interviews, thinking about the kind of work they'd like to be doing. Ronny seemed pretty anxious about all this, so I just mentioned to him that he seemed to have good rapport with people, that he was enthusiastic and friendly, so he might want to check out some of the job-training programs where he'd be working with people. Man, nearly every day for a month he'd come by here and we'd go through his whole routine. Then sure enough, one day he walked in here with a job—as an employment counselor for teens! Can you beat that! And he was beautiful at it, supervising eight other teens. You could just watch his self-esteem blossom. He was working, learning about leadership, and feeling good about his little family."

A young mother carrying her infant daughter passes in front of us and walks into the center. Two more girls run in right after her. Both are giggling. One is pregnant. Two others, a girl and a boy, brush by them in the doorway. They are holding hands. Ed continues to sweep.

"Yes, part of supporting kids is to help them realize their goals and support them in their successes. It's great when it happens and it feels good when I can, you know. But we still got to be prepared to be there for them when things don't work out, when the plan fails, when their efforts, and mine, fall through. They can become mighty discouraged and disappointed. I think growing up means you got to learn over and over again that age-old lesson, that wishin' for something isn't the same as doin' something, that you got to do what you got to do and that it takes perseverance and patience.

"Helping young people find themselves means we

got to give them some very definite things, things we all need, even when you get to be my ripe old age of forty. I'm talkin' about time, patience, empathy, respect, and acceptance. And we've got to show them things, 'cause whether we like it or not, or whether they're aware of it or not, they're lookin' for these things from us. That's why they're coming around here. That's why it's so important for us adults to keep asking ourselves, what's the teen's situation? What's he dealin' with on a day-to-day basis? What does he want for himself?

"See, we have to remember for ourselves, too, that though we might want a young fella or a young lady to make it, you know, to succeed at something, and we might be real motivated to help him, even our efforts at success aren't guaranteed. It's important for kids to know that we wrestle with those strains, too. And we got to be aware as well about what we think success might be. Our understanding of success might be different from what a kid thinks it might be for himself. Their dreams for themselves might not be our dreams for them, right? I mean, a kid might be on his way to be aspiring to be the baddest pimp, dealer, or gang leader he can be. So we got to work with that, too. You dig?

"Anyways, take Ronny, again. After a few months at his job he was laid off for reasons even beyond the control of the agency he worked for. He came right over here lookin' for me, tryin' to figure out what to do next. I tried all kinds of suggestions out on him, but he wasn't hearin' me. He was just too down. At first he seemed real interested in my ideas, but then everything sounded either bad or impossible. He was so disappointed he stopped coming to the center for weeks. That's just how he is. I'd see him sometimes when I'd be out here sweeping, but he'd just cross the street pretending we didn't see each other. So I figured he just needed some time to himself. He knew I'd be here for him when he was ready. And you know," Ed says with a wink, "he came back.

"And that's one factor that matters most definitely to these kids. I don't care what kind of adolescents you're talking about. It's that consistency, man. It's that old-time consistency they want from you. I got a couple of guys who only call me 'Steady.' Not 'Ed,' not 'Steady Eddy,' just 'Steady.' This one cat says to me, 'Hey, my man Steady! You know why I call you that? 'Cause you never change, man, not for nobody. Rock Steady.' That's what he said to me. It says a whole lot, don't it? These cats are scared you're gonna run out on 'em. Probably even expect it from you. And they're tripped out when you're really there for them.

"And the other day, man, this one young man comes up to me as I'm standing out here and puts his hand on my shoulder and says, 'Say, Ed, man, did you know I'm a father now?' That's all he said, but it blew my mind, Jack. I couldn't get this kid to do anything more than give me a grunt when I'd tell him we got a basketball game comin' up, and he loves to play. He'd grunt me a 'oh, yeah?' Not even a 'when?' or 'where?' or 'against who?' He just wouldn't express himself." Ed shakes his head and smiles. "And then he tells me, 'Ed, man, did you know I'm a father now?' I've been working with that kid for three years. Wow.

"But, you know, Dan, I have changed, though. I've been working with kids in one way or another since college. That's nearly fifteen years now. The way I used to approach the teens was by trying to put myself in their shoes, you know, like I've just been saying, to see things from their point of view, to see how they're feeling, what they're struggling with. But, damn, man, there are times these days when I find there's just no damn way I can do that; there's just no way I can bridge that age difference to get at their level and relate to where they are. Things are so different from when I was a kid, and that wasn't *that* long ago. It's not like ancient history or nothin'. But sometimes it really feels just like that; like I grew up on a different planet than these kids.

"You see, there's been a breakdown in the family, man; in the whole community, peers and all. Man, sometimes I feel I'm just so far away from what it means to be a teen in today's world." Ed sighs and moves his broom from his left hand to his right. "So what I do now is to come at 'em from where I'm at now, at age forty, and hope I can reach 'em that way.

"But the fellas and I, we end up bridging that gap all right. I think they like the fact that I'm older as opposed to younger. I think they're lookin' for somethin' they think age has got, some experience, maybe even some wisdom. These cats are hungry for that, man, let me tell you. Hmm hmm, buddy. Looking for somebody to help them through this avalanche of adolescence.

"And that's one thing I like about working with the fellas. We can have a good time together while we get into some downright heavy raps. And do the guys like to laugh! Man, that laughter's a beautiful thing. It really helps bring people together and open them up to each other. And to new ideas, too. We talk about what's on their minds. It's not my way to *make* them do anything. It's not like church where you've got to sit up straight and pay attention.

"And you see, underneath all that laughing I know they're listening, and listening real hard. Those guys are here because they're getting something from the group that they're not getting anywhere else. You ask them yourself. 'Cause you can bet your life, they wouldn't be hangin' around here if they weren't. I think the fellas know I'm accepting them where they're at. They know they can approach me with a problem or an idea and I'll listen. And I can see that same process at work when a father is expressing himself to the whole group. The rest of the guys are paying close attention to him, lettin' him know they're takin' him as seriously as I do, well, mostly. They do jive a lot.

"I want the guys to understand it's all right to be sensitive and caring. Girls ain't the only ones who can be nurturing. I want them to feel its all right if they want to play with their babies and take care of 'em, whether or not they've got a job, or whether or not they're in school, or whether or not they're still tight with their baby's mother. Sure those aspects of life can make a young man feel good about himself, as a young man and as a parent. But they're not prerequisites for wanting to love and be close with your baby. If that togetherness is there, if that parent-child bonding is going on, that's what counts. And a father will want to extend himself for his child, most definitely.

"I'm always trying to use myself as an example for whatever I'm trying to explain to the fellas. By sharing some of my experiences and feelings about different things, I let them know I can trust them and that trust is the key to openness and caring. I'll explain how I tried to solve a particular problem I had, or I'll use someone they all know, a public figure, for example, to show how he faced up to a problem and how he dealt with it. When a young man tells me he thinks he's got some kind of problem he's dealing with, I don't jump on him for being in that situation in the first place. Instead I let him know that dealing with problematic situations is part of what makes a man.

"For example, I've told the fellas how I felt when the center first opened, how I felt about being the only guy in a place full of women. They could relate to that. I've also pointed out to them that just because I saw what the problem was, that the center wasn't reaching them, didn't mean it was gonna be solved overnight.

"I can't remember how many times I had to tell the fellas that the center was as much for them as it was for the teen moms. But I found that reminding them just wasn't enough. I had to think of other ways to connect with them. That's when I decided to organize some activities I knew they'd be into, like basketball leagues, ping pong tournaments, and softball games. It seemed to work. And as I was able to get to know some of them a little better, we were able to build some definite trust between us. And I like to remind them that the fathers' group grew right out of trust. That same trust that made that one young man feel comfortable enough to talk to me about our idea of starting a fathers' group in the first place."

Ed has long since ceased sweeping. We just keep on talking.

Deep Blue Funk

I

Larry Hobbs had just turned fifteen when he felt something inside himself shut down. "The power just went off," he says to me one spring morning as we sit at a small square table in the library. "It was like I hadn't paid my 'lectric bill and then BOOM, my light was gone. Everything went black, man. Everything. Just fell out with everything and everybody. I wasn't motivated to do a damn thing."

Larry leans back in his chair, balanced on two legs, and rests his head against the wall behind him. Although he speaks quietly, his tone cracks with intensity. "I felt like the world had given up on me, so I said, 'fuck it,' 'n just gave in. Every once 'n a while I get into a funk. But, man, that one was the heaviest. I mean, a mean and bad funk. A deep blue funk. Shit, that don't even describe it, that don't even get at what I was feelin'. Man, it's a lot deeper than a funk. It goes way down deep. Down to the depths, if you know what I mean. Like some kind of syndrome or somethin', like no man's land. That's where I was. Just sittin' inside four walls, goin' nowhere, generatin' no energy. I had nothin' to do and no energy to do nothin'. I even quit runnin' with my partners for a while. I felt they weren't nothin' about nothin'. The only damn thing I felt like doin' was coppin' some bad reefer and gettin' high and stayin' high."

He stares for a moment at the magazine that lies open before him on the table. "Now take this ol' cat, will you," he says, as he leans forward and points to a large color photograph of an elderly Navajo shepherd. "Would you look at his hands. Now those are some man's hands, all right. They've got some wisdom in 'em. You can see his whole accumulated life experience right there, in all them craggly ol' wrinkles." He places a finger on the photographed hand. His young hands, like his feet, seem disproportionately large for his small but solid frame.

"Old people, man. You know, we've gotta stop trashing them. They've got a lot they can teach us. Now, I know that probably sounds real crazy comin' from a teen such as myself, but it's really true. Straight up. Older people is real important for young dudes like myself, and even for the young women. They're the ones who can show us how to do things, and when and where to do 'em at. They're the ones who should be models for us to show us what's good and bad, desirable and undesirable in life. I bet this old Indian here had someone to show him how to do things so he could feel like somebody. Bet he didn't have no deep blue funks. I remember in school this teacher tellin' us how the Indians really prepared their kids for manhood and womanhood. It was hard work, probably, you know, goin' through all them rituals and all, but at least those kids always knew there was a place for 'em and that there was somebody who was gonna help them get there. I tell ya, man, guidance. That's what it's all about, guidance. Having people around who've been there and can help you through whatever you're contendin' with. Just this morning as I was walking over here I saw this old lady. Man, it just gave me such a good feelin' to see her. I didn't talk to her or nothin', I haven't in years. But she recognized me, too, and we waved to each other." He is smiling. "She used to baby-sit me when I was real little. Just knowin' she's around and that she still remembers lets me know I still have a place in her mind.

"Now, most of my partners don't know what I'm talkin' about when I feel these things. They're always jivin' old people and makin' fun of 'em behind their backs. Maybe it's 'cause I'm changin', man. I don't know. Maybe it's 'cause they ain't. But it just seems to me that if you just look at life straight on and up front, you'd see, like I see, that being fifteen and being old, like in your fifties, or sixties, or seventies or eighties, is all pretty much the same, man.

"We're all outsiders; just outsiders lookin' for our place in this damn world of ours. For us young people it's like we've been cast out on to the sea of life, the Lake Michigan of living, all on our own, havin' to survive and find our way. And with old people, it's like they've been cast out, too, but in a different way. It's like they've been tossed out or kicked out, with the rest of the world sayin' to 'em, 'you're just too old, old man, we got no use for your tired old ways or your haggard old bones!'

"What I want to know," he says, raising his voice and pointing a finger at me, "is where do we get this idea? I mean, who gives who the almighty right to go and tell somebody he's no good, he's all washed up, he's not needed or wanted around anymore? I mean, really, man. This is down 'n out sick. Straight up cold-blooded.

"And besides, like I was sayin' before, young people and old people got a lot in common. Far as I see it, we need each other. Young people need some solid and together guidance and old folks, well, they need to be needed, too. Seems to me we ought to find some way to help each other. You know, young and old banding together." He pauses and shakes his head. "And you know why we got to band together, don't you? It's got to do with trust. Seems like all them adults in the middle don't trust either of us, the young or the old. Now how are we gonna get it together, like Ed says, if we don't trust each other and work together for all of us, all black people? No wonder the white man, no offense or nothin', Dan, is keepin' his jump on us. It's 'cause of this generational thing. Young versus adults and adults versus the old.

"Now, how 'm I supposed to get anywhere in this world with this kind of heavy action goin' down? It's been hard enough for me to pull myself out of this deep funk, man, without having to worry if there's gonna be anybody around to show me how to get through this bum trip." He pauses again. "But, maybe that's it, Dan," he says, turning his eyes toward me. "Maybe that's just it. Maybe I got in this funk in the first place because I felt I was on my own, way out there in Lake Michigan in some damn little rowboat with no kind of paddle and no kind of compass. But hey, man, I'm a survivor. I had a lot of crazy shit happen to me back then, back in the fall, and I had to realize just what had happened to me and that I needed to go hibernate for a while, cavin' in just like them bears do in the wintertime. But like I told you, man, I'm a survivor. You ask anybody. All my partners will tell you I'm a fighter. There's only so much I'll take from someone before I have to set them straight. Everyone's got their limit, and I got mine. And I'll only let someone go so far with me before I stop playing and start fighting. Man, when I was a kid, like in sixth and seventh and eighth grade, I'd be out there fighting in a second. I was little, but I was a real scrapper. I was Mr. Aggravated Battery. I came from a long line of fighters. My older brothers were fighters, too." Larry hesitates for a moment as he scratches his head. "I lost my oldest brother in a fight when I was in seventh grade. I remember thinking, shit, I lost my brother in a damn knife fight over some kind of bullshit."

"Did that make you stop fighting?" I ask.

"No, not at first. That's for sure. If anything, it made me more angry and more hateful. My fighting became even crazier: bottles, bats, rocks, anything I could get my hands on. I would get real wild. Sometimes I'd even be unaware of who I was fighting or why we started up in the first place. I'd get so angry when I was fighting I'd get even stronger 'cause I was so mad.

"That's one thing I really wish I had, someone to show me how to control it. I've got one mean temper, boy. If I'm pushed far enough I'll go off like a .38. Boom! I'll explode. And when I go off, brother, watch out 'cause I stop thinking. I really lose my cool and I won't know what the hell I'll be doing. That's how this whole funk thing started, man.

"You see, I was suspended from school back in the

fall. I was just standing in the hall doin' a little 'business' with my partners and this assistant principal, some white lady, came by and told me to move along down the hallway. So I just stood there with my friends holding my ground. I wasn't hurtin' nobody. And then she said, 'All you black kids are all alike. You don't do what you're told to do.' Well, Jack, you know that shit didn't go down too well with me. And I went off, 'You white rancid bitch!' Then she asked me for my ID and I threw the fuckin' thing at her. Man, I fired that card at her as hard as I could from about as far away as you are from me." He reaches his arms out across the table. "I was so fuckin' angry at her, and at my friends, too. They were saying junk to me like, 'Hey man, you gonna take that shit? You gonna let her say that to you?' The pressure was just too much and I went off. They told me to come back to school a couple of months later, but I told them to stuff it. School is runt, anyways. And I've been out ever since.

"And that week I quit my job, too. I was sick and tired of working for some white man. Let the white man earn *my* respect, is what I thought. I was tired of being a nobody to them. And I'll be real honest with you, I'll tell you something about black people. Man, we're not as dumb as the white man thinks. No way. What it is is that the white man had done all that he could to keep us down 'n dumb. That's why I know cats like Ed can relate to me. 'Cause he's black, too. And he knows what we're up against without me havin' to explain it to him like I do to people like you."

"That's not fair," I protest.

"Look, man, I appreciate you wantin' to talk with

me. You're an all right dude and I know you care about us here. I wouldn't be talkin' to you if I didn't think so. But the fact of the matter is you ain't black and I is. So there's some stuff you'll never understand, especially if guys like me don't lay it out for you. You dig?"

"I dig."

"That's why Our Place is all right, man. It's the one place I know about where there are adults who want to listen to you and give you some guidance. I wouldn't be comin' here if I didn't think so, I'll tell you that. You see, here people are willin' to trust you, they're willin' to accept me as myself, Larry Hobbs. But we need a lot more of it out there. There's just too many young people out in those streets looking for the same thing I'm lookin' for, a place to be somebody.

He sighs.

"I only wish my girl friend's mother knew as much. I guess that's part of what I've been trying to tell ya, about this funk I've been in. You see, I'm gonna be a father in about seven weeks and that means some heavy responsibility. But I'm ready for it. I've just got to be. I feel real strong about doing right by my child and his mother.

"I've had to do a whole lot of growing in the last few months, man, and I've been going through some changes my partners just can't relate to. I've had to go way beyond them. I just don't got the time to be messin' around with them, hangin' out and jivin' on the street corner. They can't relate to where I'm at, and that's not out of any fault of their own, it's just that they ain't in my shoes. I've got to be about a man's business. Right now I'm holdin' down two jobs. Most of my friends can't even stick with one. But I don't blame some of 'em. If I wasn't gonna be a father right soon I'd probably be runnin' around like they is.

"But things are different for me. And I've got to accept that. Sometimes it gets to feeling strange. I know I'm still young, but I've got a man's, a real man's job to do now. And I'm feelin' bigger 'cause of it. I've got a lot to learn right quick, too. But responsibility isn't new for me. Shit, from jump street I had to take responsibility for things. And I mean from the beginning. I've been going with Sherelle for nearly four years now and when we decided to make love I took her down here to see Nurse Todd at the clinic to get some birth control pills. So, since she had them I thought things were, you know, cool. But she got pregnant not too long after we started having sex together. She didn't take the pills. Can you believe that?" he asks, with his eyes open wide. "She didn't even take them. I still can't believe it.

"I'll never understand totally what goes on in that woman's head. We talked and talked for nearly two months after we found out she was pregnant about what we were going to do. At the time no one else knew. I guess we just waited too long for an abortion. I sort of pushed for her to have the baby. I just couldn't see killing it. I figured that was wrong, as far as my own values go. Actually, I guess she would have had an abortion if we had acted sooner. But we didn't have the money, anyways. I told you I checked that out, too. I called some hospitals, I came here and talked to Nurse Todd and Mrs. Henry. I laid the whole thing out for them. But I just didn't have that kind of money. It costs so much, nearly eight hundred dollars. And we sure couldn't bring it to our folks, least that's how we saw it at first. Then her mother catches wind of this through the grapevine and, man, was she mad! I don't know how she found out my schedule, but she called me at home one morning and talked to me for a good twenty minutes or more. She was furious. I mean, red hot and steaming furious. She and Sherelle had had it out and Sherelle ran away from home and came to stay with me and my family for about two weeks. Then, one day her mother calls me and invites me over for dinner. Can you dig that? Invites *me* to dinner."

"Did Sherelle go, too?"

"No, she stayed home at my place. When I got there I was already wired, man. Like real nervous. I didn't know what to expect 'cause I knew she was still real mad. They all wanted to sit down and eat but I just couldn't man. So I said, 'You know, this may not be the right time for you, but I got to talk now, before I can eat a thing.' So we started talking and I says to her mother, 'Why don't you pay for the abortion and I'll pay you back.' I must have been so scared that I actually asked her to do it! Well, I don't have to tell you, she didn't like that idea no how. '*You* pay *me* back!' " Larry says, imitating Sherelle's mother. " 'Where are you going to get the money to pay me back? You don't work, do you? 'Cause if you did, you'd have some money to pay for this. No sir, I don't trust you.'

"Man, when she said that to me, that just changed everything. I felt really, really low. Shit, I've been going with her daughter for nearly four years! Doesn't that mean anything? It was like I wasn't worth shit. 'I don't trust you,' he mimicks again. "Just cast out like I was dirt, like I didn't matter, like I didn't have feelings.

Deep down inside I knew I had to win her trust and prove myself to her if things were going to be all right in the future. Whew! There I was, man, suspended from school, way deep off in this funk, out of work, my woman's pregnant and I'm about to be a father. And to top it off, her mother tells me, 'I don't trust you.' It was like I was set on fire. And I knew the only way to prevent myself from being burned even more was to get myself together and get responsible."

Larry leans back and sighs. "Seven weeks to go."

II

Word had been out for a few days by the time Larry swung by Our Place for the Wednesday night fathers' group. He has just become the father of six-pound, two-ounce Claude Sterling Hobbs. This is Larry's first visit to the center since Claude Sterling had come into the world. From father-to-be to father. His status has changed overnight.

The whole center seems to twitch with anticipation of his arrival, me included. He enters through the front door with a lilt in his walk. His broad smile radiates ease. His eyes, although glazed from exhaustion, beam with pride. A hero's welcome! Hands extend from all directions. Hands shake in congratulations. Hands shake heartily in return. Larry seems overwhelmed and overjoyed by his reception. His shoelaces, though, remain untied. His trademark. Not everything has changed.

The center is crowded and Larry's arrival only fuels the already frantic pace at which the teens are cooking, feeding their babies, and talking informally in small groups. The teen mothers have been preparing food all afternoon for both the fathers' club and their own teen mothers' support group. Between six-thirty and seven o'clock most of the fathers come by the center. Some grab a plate of food. Laughter, babies' cries, and pots clanging in the kitchen whirl and blend with the disco rhythms beating from the radio in a symphony of human hustle and chatter.

By seven o'clock, most of the fathers are lounging in the parents' room. Some are still eating. Arms and legs sprawl over all available couches and chairs. Ed closes the door. It is quieter now. The girls are in another room, in their group. The babies are with the child-care staff. A palpable sense of relief fills the room. By setting themselves apart from the others, the fathers have given their identity and status some formal definition. Their posture is theirs by choice, not by conscription or accusation. The room is theirs, at least for the next two hours.

"Say there, Larry, how's the realm of fatherhood suitin' you these days?" Lewis asks.

"Tripped out, man. Tripped out. It's been all hustle since my son was born."

"Hmm hmm," a voice agrees. Ed nods also.

"Dig this," Larry says, "Sherelle had that little baby on the day of her baby shower. I figure she just got so excited, you know, all the presents and all. Man, these people sure helped us out a lot. Otherwise we'd be spending some tall paper, if you know what I mean. At the time, I was over at her crib, but I had run out to the store to get stuff for the shower and when I got back over there her friends said that she'd been rushed off to the hospital 'cause she was about to have her baby.

Man, let me tell you, when I heard that, I dropped everything and I mean literally, everything. Just BAM," he says, dropping his arms to dramatize his point. "And I ran to that hospital, I ran the whole way. No such thing as a red light that afternoon, Jack!"

"I heard that!" Thomas calls out.

"So, I go to this room where Sherelle is and she's in there just waitin' for the baby to come. I can see the baby's head just buddin' out from between her legs."

"Oh, Lord!" someone shouts.

"You know, from her hole. Man when I saw that, it just blew my mind. No shit. I was trippin' out on that one, boy, for sure." He stares ahead at the wall and shakes his head. He then looks at Ray and then at me. "I just couldn't believe what I was seeing. I mean, whoa, Jack, that head, that little round part, you know, the top of the head. Well, it was just pushing itself out ever so much from her 'gina, man. I just couldn't handle it. And you know I had to go cool out in the chapel and think this one out!"

"On your knees, boy!" commands Robert, as the others laugh. Charles drops to his knees, quivering as if he were Larry. "Oh, Lord, you just got to help me. This little itty bitty head was just stickin' out of her you-know-what."

"No joke," Larry insists. "I was really overcome by the whole thing. My baby was being born and all I knew was that I felt like praying."

"A-men!" Lewis cheers.

"Lord knows when I last felt like I really wanted to go to chapel and pray, but I sure did that day. I felt overcome, you know, just filled up with thanks and gratitude to somebody, or something, or some super force that helped shape the changes I've gone through in the last six or seven months. Something sure has been helpin' me get myself together for my son and Sherelle in terms of my responsibilities and my work."

"Now that's a word I want to talk about," Ardis says, "responsibility."

"What do you want to say about it?" Ed asks.

"I don't rightly know, but, man, I know this whole responsibility rap has got some very definite problems to it. Sometimes I feel it's all a set up. Like we was being framed, or something."

"That's it," Lewis agrees. "You're right on time." His response is quiet, steady and even, taking his time to make sure of what he wants to say. "Now, if you ask me for my personal views on the matter, I'd say we're treated like we ain't nothin' but a bunch of outcasts, society's young outlaws."

"Straight up. We definitely got the short end of the stick," Ardis continues. "All this talk about helping the teen father ain't nothin' but just that—just a lot of talk. This ain't no new deal, man. It's the same ol' thing: a raw deal."

" 'N no one is interested in how I feel about getting a girl pregnant 'n becomin' a father 'n all, least of all my girl friend's family," Lewis explains.

"Or a girl gettin' you to get her pregnant," Freddie adds. My eyes turn to Larry. He leans forward in his chair toward Freddie, as if he hopes Freddie will say more. "I want to know who's responsibility is the birth control?"

"Hold on to that a second, I'll get to that in a minute," Lewis says. "Like I was sayin', they're makin' it real clear I'm not wanted around, like I didn't exist or somethin'. What do they think is gonna happen? Just because they're trying to ignore me don't mean I'm gonna up and disappear like this here smoke," he says, pausing to take a drag from his cigarette. "Shit, they won't let me come over and visit my daughter, not even with other people around. What do they think I'm gonna do, drop her on the floor or something?"

"Knowing you, they probably think you'll go 'n use her for shootin' hoop," Karl retorts from his corner across the room. Everyone laughs.

"All right, all right, you guys," Lewis pleads with a trace of a smile. "But seriously, now, not all dudes are ignorant or unwillin' to learn about little babies and how to take care of 'em." He looks around the room to see if the other fathers are still following him.

"I heard that," says Richard, an athletic seventeen-year-old who usually keeps pretty much to himself. "But with me it's my family that's puttin' the pressure on to stay away from my daughter and her mother."

" 'N just 'cause me 'n my daughter's mother had us a fallin' out a while back don't mean I'm any less the father, 'n it don't mean they should be keepin' me from my own flesh 'n blood," Lewis asserts.

Richard looks over at Lewis. "It's the same trip, man. They don't want me goin' over there 'n spendin' time. If you ask me, they wouldn't even have me spendin' any money on the baby if they had their own way 'bout things. They just want me to steer clear of that whole scene. It's like they're trying to deny the fact that I'm a father or somethin'."

Lewis replies. "I hear what you're contendin' with. Seems like we're all gettin' it one way or the other. I'm tellin' you, I've got a lot of responsibilities to uphold that sometimes I wish I didn't have. Hey, I know I'm no angel or nothin' . . . "

"No shit," ribs another father.

"Well, I mean, I'm just tryin' to be honest, man. There's plenty of times I'm runnin' from 'em, too. Just seems like no one's willin' to help me out or show me how the hell I'm supposed to do what everyone expects me to do. It's like they think I'm born with that kind of knowledge, wisdom, and understandin'.

"And then, on top of that, society's tellin' you the guy is supposed to do all the providin' for his family. Now, how the hell am I supposed to do that when I'm not taken seriously and they don't want me interferin' with the baby? Just 'cause I ain't livin' with my baby and her mother together under one roof don't mean we still ain't a family. No, I ain't married, but neither is divorced parents. Married or not, my daughter's got herself a daddy and married or not I got myself a daughter."

The room is quiet for a moment.

"I'll bet I'm tellin' it straight," Lewis adds, "probably all of us in this very room feel as if we're made to be the villains in this scene, straight up. I know I got responsibilities. Everyone's tellin' me that all the time. But I got me some rights, too; like the right to be taken seriously as I try to get myself together, don't I?"

"You know what's all right about this here fathers' group," Ronny states as he leans forward in his seat. "it's that you ain't pressured or hassled to do this or that, or think this or think that. Shit, I get enough of that jive during the other twenty-four. I mean, I know I got things to do I don't really want to do. But like I usually say, that's just part of life. But what I can't dig is when people be puttin' too many demands on you, expectin' you to be doin' things that is really out of your control.

"I guess it's that control thing that gets to me, man. Like with that job I had, one minute I had it, the next one I don't. No one asked me if I was tired of workin' there. No, but because of the man's damn decision somewhere up top, I lost my job. And I wasn't alone, either. There was others who lost their jobs, too.

"Man, I'm just sick and tired of havin' other people decide how my life gets run. Maybe, the best thing I can do is to get myself into college, get me some down collateral, and get me a good job so I won't be waitin' on the man's decision."

"That sounds mighty good to me, young man," Ed says with a nod. "Now, when you get out of college and land yourself a good job, don't forget about me if *I* come to *you* for a job someday!"

"Now, how 'bout that birth control?" Freddie questions, "they can't be pinnin' that rap on us, too."

"What do you mean?" Ed asks.

"Hey, man, they be tryin' to stick us with every other problem about teen pregnancy."

"Yeah, buddy."

"My straight up opinion is that a girl's gotta watch out for herself. She's got to be wise about the world, if you know what I mean. She's the one who's gonna carry that thing around in her big ol' belly for nine months and then have to care for it 'n raise it. Self-protection, I say. No chick should be waitin' for some dude to say, 'Oh dear, have you prepared yourself with the proper birth control devices so that we may engage in sexual intercourse?' No way, brother. She's got to be *ready* for when things get hot and *heavy*!"

"Tell it!"

"How 'bout the rest of you fellas?" Ed asks. "How 'bout you, Donald?"

"That's part of it." His answer is short, his tone curt.

Ed tries again to draw Donald out. "What do you mean by that, brother?"

"Like I said, that's part of it."

"Oh, he don't want to answer," Larry says. "I agree but not totally. Straight up, a girl's got to protect herself. But if the dude is about the kind of stuff he should be about, and by that I mean being a man, he'd be sure to find some way of making sure his woman is taken care of in terms of some control."

"So you're sayin' both the partners, male and female, have to take responsibility?"

"That's it, Ed. She's dumb if she don't, and he ain't no kind of man if he don't. Actually, man, if I had been truly thinking, I mean, if I had been really giving things the old twenty-four-hour check, I might not have ended up with this new lifetime bill. I admit it, man, I was selfish. I didn't take any precautions to protect *myself*. You know, just a little bit extra, just in case. But that's the thing, man, about sex. You're into doin', not thinkin'."

Freddie laughs. "Doin', not thinkin'! Ain't *that* the truth!"

"It's everywhere you look, man," Larry goes on to say. "I bet I've probably seen some kind of sex nearly every day of my life, even if it's just seein' some dude grab some ass as he's walkin' down the street. Booty, man. For real. All I know is I wanted some hands-on action myself, to see what it was like."

"Okay. So you're talking about a kind of group responsibility," Ed says, "lookin' out for each other, you might say. Now ain't that what a family's all about? Helpin' each other out, and not bein' left out there on your own? So when we're talkin' about manhood and being young men, it's hard to keep it separate from talkin' about womanhood."

"And childhood," Ardis quickly adds.

"And childhood. Most definitely. Now what does manhood mean to you fellas?"

For a moment, the fathers are quiet.

"Power," says one.

"Being on top," claims another.

"Getting what you need to make it," answers a third.

"All right," Ed says. "Power, being on top, making it. Good. What else?"

"Responsibility."

"Bringing home the bacon."

"Good, but for who? Makin' it and bein' responsible for who?"

"For yourself."

"Just yourself?"

"For your children, your woman, and your whole family," Larry answers with conviction. "We just can't be thinkin' of only our own individual selves."

"Wanna bet?" Freddie laughs.

"C'mon, man. We've got to be thinkin' of all of us. That's why we're here with Ed, right? Tryin' to figure this out for ourselves individually and communally. This, out-for-your-individual-self thing is a straight up bum trip. That how the man would want us to act. But we've got to be about the business of lending your fellow man a helping hand. That's how us blacks pull each other down, we out doin' each other in, not helpin' each other out. It's all about stickin' together. That's where the power lies; stickin' together and buildin' pride."

"Let me tell you somethin' 'bout responsibility," Freddie says. He seems serious now. "Responsibility is bein' able to take care of yourself. Now, Dan, you remember when I was makin' some tea for myself back there in the kitchen?"

"Yeah."

"That's responsibility. Straight up. I did it all on my own." He winks. "It's easy, you just put some water in a pan 'n boil it. And, look, there's nothin' to clean. I can fend for myself just fine. I won't be needin' no wife to cook for me. I cook fine for myself already. And probably better 'n most women anyhow. I'll be doin' the cookin' for my wife when I get married. When *she* comes home from work, *I'll* be the one havin' the dinner ready."

"Now, how's you gonna have time to cook 'n have everything ready when your ol' lady comes home, when you're out workin' all day?" Thomas asks.

"Easy, man. I'll just be *lookin'* for work," he answers with a straight face. "She'll be the one who's really workin'. While she's workin', I'll be cookin'. 'N while I'll be cleanin', she'll be workin'. And while she be workin', I be washin'. And while I be *lookin'* for work, she be *doin'* the work.

"I'll have the diapers changed, the babies' bottoms rubbed and their bellies fed, too. Looks like I'm gonna be one of them whatyamacallits—'househusbands.' "

"Now ain't that a trip!" Ed says with a laugh.

"Y'alls on a trip, I swear," Robert declares, speaking for the first time. "My contention is that the black woman is probably the backbone of things. I've got to hand it to 'em. They do a downright good job at keepin' things together. At least when they get older." He shakes his head as he begins to raise his voice. "But these younger ones," he continues, pointing toward the room where the teen mothers are meeting, "they're all about nothin'. Well, maybe not all of 'em, but there's sure plenty of them young girls who don't do nothin' but talk a lot of junk; just gabbin' and gossipin' and carryin' on like they don't got a brain in their silly ol' head. Straight up." He is now waving his arms. "Now don't get me wrong, fellas, I think the womenfolk is outasight, if you know what I mean." He winks, too. "But there ain't a dame I wouldn't smash in a minute. I wouldn't forget that I'm one of you fellas."

Ardis looks angry. "Now don't you be talkin' that trash about smashin' people, man. That ain't nothin' but a lot of junk, too. I've seen too much of that kind of jive in my day. This smashin' shit is shit. Hey, now that's one thing I ain't never gonna do is hit my kids. My son is two and a half and I ain't hit him yet. Neither has his mother. I don't got no kind of time to sit around 'n listen to this smashin' people shit. Forget that. That's how ol' folks think things should be done. Just 'cause they do 'em like that way down South don't mean we got to be doin' it up here, too.

"Look, I've been on my own since I was thirteen and I've learned how a dude's got to live in this world to get by. When you're born black, you've got to be prepared to go either way, if you know what I mean," he says, moving his hand slowly in front of his body and then back again. "You've got to be a fencewalker. You know what I mean? Either side and both sides. Sometimes both sides at once. Straddling the line, brother, is what it's all about. The legal and the illegal.

"It's tough out there and it's gonna be gettin' even tougher. So why make life even tougher for little kids. There's no reason why we got to stop 'em and jack 'em up or belt 'em like I was. That don't teach 'em anything but to be angry 'n violent. That'll be all they know. Instead of whuppin' 'em, parents ought to show their young'uns the ways of the street so they know how to survive on either side of the line. We've got to love the little ones, not be smashin' them."

"Say, I wasn't talkin' about smashin' no little children," Robert says in his own defense.

"I know that."

"But now that you mention it," Robert continues, "I think kids need a good whuppin' now and again. How else is they supposed to know what's wrong and right? You got to let them know. I mean, how else is they gonna know when they're misbehavin'? Sometimes you can't just talk to a little child or baby figurin' you're gonna be explainin' everythin' to 'em; they're just too young for that. So you got to have other means of communication, if you know what I mean?"He points to his belt. "Hey, I sure didn't like it when I was catchin' it, but I know I probably needed it, though. And if I think my kids'll need it, I sure won't hesitate."

"Now ain't that child abuse?" someone shouts.

"Hey, I ain't talkin' no child abuse here neither. All I'm sayin' is that kids need some discipline; it's just part of what they need to grow up right. Naw, I ain't talkin' about no child abuse; that shit is when you start throwin' 'em against walls and burnin' 'em on purpose 'n stuff. What I'm talkin' about is different; I remember my mama tellin' me she wouldn't be doin' it if she didn't care about me. It shows kids you care for 'em.''

"Y'all ain't seen nothin'," Karl exclaims, "till you've seen my grandmother, boy, whowee! Could she raise the dead with a whuppin'! I remember this one night, my grandmother wanted me to do something and I said, 'no.' Well, I did 'n I saw her start to come after me, so I grabbed the belt off the wall so she couldn't use it on me. And do you know what she did? She went upstairs 'n got an old pipe 'n come after me with it. Whowee, did I run. Run right out the house into the snow with no shoes on!''

Ardis stands and walks to another chair. He sits down. "That smashin' stuff is still a lot of smack. First, it's smashin' your girl friend, then it's smashin' your kids. Smashin' ain't nothin' but smashin'.'' He turns to the rest of the group. "And I'll tell you all something. You know why I love little children? 'Cause when you're their age, you'll never experience love like you did then, and by showin' kids you care for them and love them, they'll keep that care and love in 'em in their eyes, for their whole lives. Just by lookin' at a person's eyes, I can tell if they was loved when they was a child. I definitely believe in that old saying, 'Do unto others as you want them to do onto you.'

"You see this scar here by my eye?" Ardis says, pointing to it.

"Ali!" someone shouts.

"I got this one about a week ago when I was in this fight, 'n let me tell you, scar or no scar, I'd fight that guy again if I could. Shit, the only ones who should be smashed are the ones who would smash little children or anybody smaller than themselves. This dude I fought, man, was a close partner of mine. We used to talk and smoke and all and do all kinds of junk together. We definitely rode together, man. The cat is married to my older sister.

"The other day she tells me he was beatin' on my little three-year-old nephew." Ardis is now walking about the room, pacing anxiously as he talks. "I tried to talk to the man first, but I guess he thought I was weak 'cause I was tryin' to talk with him 'n work things out without gettin' into all kinds of heavy violence. But to this cat, man, if you're a talker, you ain't no man. Tryin' to talk things through to some folks is what they call 'abnormal behavior.' To them, women talk and men fight. Simple. This guy just read me wrong, 'cause he started grabbin' me and chokin' me and jackin' on me, and at this point I just said, this is crazy, and I started firing back on him and I just got so mad all I could think of was grabbin' what I could. So I found this bottle and cracked him over the head with it. Bam. I didn't want to really hurt the man or get myself hurt or get into any kind of trouble, if you know what I mean, 'cause I'm into martial arts and I could hurt someone very seriously. I mean what kind of man are you if you go 'round beatin' on little children?"

Ardis shakes his head. "I don't know, if it was me that was doin' crazy shit like beatin' on somebody else's kid, or even my own, I'd expect someone to come by and blow me away. Straight up 'n kill me.

"Listen, man, I remember being beaten on by my sisters and my father. I hated it then and I hate it now.

Like zero respect for it, man. It can make me real mad. That's why I think I grew up with this mean streak inside me."

"I used to have me a stubborn streak, too," Karl interrupts. "I'd do just what I wanted to do and figured if I was bigger and stronger than the other person it was them and not me that would have to change his tune. They was always tellin' me when I was a kid that I'd end up like my daddy. I guess I was sort of like him. I was the one who'd speak his mind. I was sort of bullheaded, I guess. But when they'd say that to me I would get so mad. The hell if I was going to end up like my father. He killed two people and spent most of my younger life in prison."

"He still there?" Charles asks.

"Naw, he's out now. They let him out, self-defense. You just take a guess how many times he's been shot up. Go ahead and guess."

"Six."

"Four."

"A hundred."

"Swiss cheese, man!"

"Way off, way off, man. He's been shot about fourteen or fifteen or sixteen times all over his body. Straight up," Karl informs us as he points to parts of his body to show us where the bullets had found their mark.

"I told you, Swiss cheese, man," Freddie says again.

Karl tries to ignore Freddie's crack. "No way was I gonna be like him. I'd get so goddamn mad every time they'd say that to me, I'd go off and cry. I really resented that stuff. I've always been the independent

sort and I was going to be damned if I'd let them tell me
who or what I was goin' to be."

Ardis speaks again. "My family would hardly listen
to me at all or let me say my piece when it was my turn
to talk. It made me mad. But I just usually handle it."

"How?" Ed asks.

"By talking, man. Just like I'm doin' right now. By
talking about it."

"I'm hip to what you're sayin' 'bout talkin',"
Thomas says affirmingly. "Me, I try to reveal myself
mostly to women."

"A sweet-talkin' ladies' man!" Freddie cracks.

"See," Thomas says, pointing at Freddie, "guys just
don't understand what I got to say, so I rap to the
women. To my mother, and people I think really care
and want to know about me. Now, there's some crazy
people out there who think they know me, you know,
the way I am out there on the street, but that's not the
only thing that I'm about. And they think they know
me." His chuckle belies his sarcasm.

"You see," Ardis explains, "this is a different side of
me than many people think I got. I can talk about
myself 'n spend a lot of time thinkin' about all kinds of
shit that's goin' on in my life and I try to understand it."

"That's beautiful, man," Ed replies.

"Did I ever tell you I'm gonna write a book, too, one
day?" Ardis continues, "I'm gonna call my book 'The
Wishing Well.' It's gonna be a book about psychology.
Back at home we've got all these books on religion and
psychology. And you know I love to read. Read all the
time. Never made it past ninth grade in high school, but
I love to read. I think I've always thought about

psychology and people; it's just how I think. The psychology of the mind, the ways people relate to each other. It's a tripped-out body of knowledge. Ever read a book called *The Prophet*? A guy named Gibran, or whoever, wrote it. For real. It talks about our inner and outer selves and relatin' to other people. You see, what I figure is I'll get my GED and then go to a junior college, check things out a bit from the inside and then go to regular college. My mind loves to learn. That's right, you just put me out there and I'm just like one big ol' sponge, soakin' it all in, brother," he says as he laughs. "Like I said, I've been on my own ever since I was thirteen, man. And havin' to think for myself when I was very young. I've lived in the cold streets during the winter with no place to go. I've lived in hotels, motels, everywhere. But I survived because I wanted to learn, and I was good at it, too, Jack. Hey, man, at thirteen I learned how to change five dollars into fifty dollars. I learned all about walkin' the line. I know the ways of the street. Right now, my life goals and objectives is that I want to get into psychology, like I said. And after that to get a degree in something else, maybe business or something, and then after that to get me at least one more degree, man, I'm gonna get all these different degrees to develop my mind."

"Like I was sayin'," Thomas resumes as he nods toward Ardis, "There's just all these people who don't understand or don't take the time or interest to try 'n understand who I am and what I got to say about anything. The trouble is trying to express myself. Sometimes others just can't understand what I'm talkin' about, 'cause they haven't been through what I've personally been through. Usually it's that they just haven't settled down enough to listen and hear me out. Sometimes I think I could talk for hours, man. That's why I like to paint."

"Paint?" Freddie says bewildered. "Since when you been paintin'?"

"Paintin' is a trip, man. Look over there," Thomas announces, turning to the wall near the window. "Those three paintin's over there in the corner are mine. Mrs. Henry hung 'em up for me."

"The man's got some talent," Charles says. "How 'bout you paintin' a portrait of me. Which side do you think is my good side? This side? Or this side?"

"Your backside!" Freddie fires back.

"Really," Thomas insists, trying not to let the banter distract him, "doin' those things helps me express myself. And I guess I'm just one of those people that's got to be expressing himself. Talkin', man. That's what it's all about. Talkin', talkin', talkin'. I really learn about myself when I'm talkin'."

"Who told you to say that?" Freddie jokes, still wanting to be playful.

"Nobody, man, that's just the straight-up way I see things. Somehow by talkin' and havin' to think about one thing or another really intensely, I seem to put things together for myself that I never thought before. Yes, I've got all kinds of Thomas Richieness in me to get out, to talk out. And it's especially important since I've got this court date comin' up and, brother, do I have to get my shit together by that day!" Everyone, including Thomas, cracks up when he says that. "So, Ed, man," he continues while still laughing, "you and me gotta meet real soon, okay? I've got to get my thoughts in shape for the big bout."

Ed nods.

After the laughter quiets down, Larry speaks. "That's just it, Ed. I need some help, too, for my big bout. 'Cause I've got to be about the business of helpin' my little son have a good role model he can look up to. See, I'm afraid he won't have one, a real good one, in me. I'd do anything to be somebody he can look up to. You know, for the guidance a child needs. I really want to provide for my little family; provide the green stuff and the love we need to survive in this world. Now, I've only been a father officially for a few days, but I've been tryin' to get it together for a long time now and I just feel that I'm not doin' enough, that I'm gonna let my little son down when he might need me most. You know, fail him."

Ed looks surprised. "What do you think you should be doing that you're not?" he asks. "You're even holding down two gigs."

"I don't know exactly," Larry replies, "I think that because I'm a father, I feel I should be doin' what real fathers, you know, older fathers do. I know I'm only sixteen, but that's besides the point, man. I'm a father and I can accept that, I'm proud of it. I love my little family, like I said, but sometimes I can already feel the pressures are too much. I feel I have to do more and more when deep down inside I know I can't do any more, at least for right now. Sometimes it's like I'm already at the limit, man. But then again, I think if I were a good father, I'd be doin' more for my son, that I'd always be tryin' to do more and more." Larry stops to catch his breath and collect his thoughts. "How am I supposed to know when 'more' is enough?"

"Sounds to me like you're doin' plenty there, Larry," Ed says. "You're working, you're concerned about your baby's welfare, you're conscientious about your responsibilities. Now, don't lose track of all those good things you're into. Don't be tryin' to take on more than what you feel comfortable doin'. As all you fellas know, bein' a father carries with it some very definite responsibilities, but being a teen father doesn't mean that you have to carry all the responsibilities in life. I'm sure many of you guys have felt overwhelmed at times by all you think is expected of you, like Larry here. Maybe that's why some of you find it real difficult to be a father sometimes."

"Right on," Richard confirms from his cross-legged seat on the couch.

"Okay, so you know what I'm talkin' about," Ed continues. "Be gradual in the kinds and amounts of responsibility you take on. You know when you feel like you're OD'ing on responsibility. If you're feeling some pretty heavy pressure from your family or from your young lady's family, see if you can talk it out with them. This is a time in your life when you're learning how to accept responsibilities, and I definitely think you're getting it together. Truly, man."

"But, Ed," Larry breaks in. "I asked you when is 'more' enough? How do I know when I'm doin' enough?"

"Hey, man, you answered that question yourself. You said it when you said, I'm at the limit. Listen to yourself, Larry, and you, too, fellas, and trust what you hear inside yourself. There are just some things you can't do now but will later on, at some other point. This is the beginning for you, not the end. As time goes on, you'll be doin' plenty more. Don't worry. Ain't that right, Dan?"

"That's right."

"You know," Ed says, "in an odd way, bein' a new parent is sort of like being a child. It's all a part of a developing process. Like your son, for example. He's got to sit up before he can crawl, and crawl before he can walk, and walk before he can run. You hear what I'm sayin'?"

Larry sits silently for a moment, then gives an understanding nod. "I hear you," he says.

III

A chill autumn wind. An overcast sky. Small pools and puddles of rainwater dot the streets and sidewalks. From Church Street to Darrow to Foster to Ridge to Central to Sheridan Road, Larry and I weave a course north and east from Our Place to Lake Michigan. A father for five months now, feeling pride, pressure, satisfaction, strain, and anger. Meeting bills and meeting needs, with expectations accelerating beyond his control and that angers him further. It also embarrasses him.

We stand quietly facing the great lake.

"Some little spot, eh, Dan? Sure seems peaceful out here." He sighs. "Seems so far away from everything that's goin' on back there. I just had to get outta there, man, away from that center, away from Sherelle, away from all them people back there in Evanston."

He laughs. "Sounds funny, don't it, back there in

Evanston? Sure feels like we're in a different world out here. Shit, for all I care, right now we might as well be in a different world." Larry trudges through the sand toward the water's edge and I follow him.

"This is the spot I come to when I gotta cool out and think a lot of things through, man. Not too many people I know know about this place, so I'm usually pretty safe out here, in terms of not bein' hassled and bein' left alone with my thinkin'. Sometimes Evanston just seems too small for me, like I'm livin' in this little box and when I try and stand up I smack my head against the top. But as you can tell, there's plenty of room for me out here. Did you know on a clear day you can see all the way down to Gary? And I'd swear, sometimes even across to Michigan. Straight up. Lots of room to breathe out here." He gazes at the lake. "You know that camera I got?"

"The one your uncle suggested you buy?"

"Yeah, sometimes I come out here with it to take pictures. My uncle says I got my knack for takin' pictures from him. He's real good. Been takin' pictures from way back. He's helped me out a lot with learnin' about cameras and photography. But usually I just take pictures of people. Mostly Sherelle and Claude Sterling. Man, I've got rolls of film of them two. She's got 'em now for safekeepin'."

He reaches down, picks up a pebble and throws it far out into a crowd of crashing waves.

"But after what went down with her a couple of weeks ago, I don't know if I'll ever see them pictures again."

"Why, what happened?" I ask.

"You mean you ain't heard about the fight we had!" he says with disbelief. "I was afraid everybody'd caught up with that one."

"I heard something about it."

"Well, there ain't much to it, man. I just went off at her. That's why you ain't seen me at the center for two weeks. I just can't go by there no more, least for a while. And that's hard, too, man, 'cause I know I want to go by there and see her but I know I gotta keep some definite distance on that scene. And that's too bad for a lot of reasons. I used to think of Our Place as a kind of home, man. I mean me and Sherelle, we ain't adults yet or anything and can't walk around like we're in adult shoes, but we'd try to make 'em fit as best we could. We couldn't live together in our own place or nothin', but we've done just about everythin' else in terms of bein' adults as far as, you know, males and females are concerned.

"So when I'd come over to the center to see Sherelle at the end of the day after we've both been workin' at our respective jobs. I'd feel as if I was comin' home to see her and my son. And I'd like to think that my woman would be glad to see me, too, you know. I wouldn't be expectin' her to drop everythin' she was doin' but somehow to let me know in those special ways she's got, that she was glad to see me. I'd want to feel like I was comin' home after a long hard day at work bringin' home the green and wantin' to be greeted by my family."

He looks at me. "But I was feelin' real frustrated, man. Real frustrated. I could feel her movin' away from me, not all at once, but slowly. At first I just figured she didn't have the time to see me 'cause of

Claude Sterling. And I could understand that. Sherelle's a good woman and a good mother and I want my son to have that kind of attention. Then she'd say she was busy with her girl friends. All of a sudden they're more important than seeing me. And now dig this, she and her mother are startin' to get real close. Can you believe that? Man, all of a sudden she's able to relate to her mother." He was shaking his head. "And where do you think that leaves me?"

"On the outside?" I offer.

"You bet. On the outside, just like I was tellin' you. I don't know what's with her mother, man. Sometimes I think she's actually opening up to me. Like I called her once when me and Sherelle were having a problem. I was ready to give up on her and even on the baby. I mean I'd keep supportin' him financially and all, but really I'd just give up. But she said not to. I felt she was listening to me. I hadn't seen her in about a month, but when I talked to her, she seemed like she was more open to me. I just had that feeling. She used to listen to me, but I could tell she didn't care. But this time I could tell she really did care about *me*.

"Then, just a little while after that I was over at their house and at ten-thirty she came to me and said, 'It's time for you to get out.' Man, she blew me away. I didn't expect it, but I should have. She hasn't really accepted me yet. No how. Despite all I've done for her daughter and her grandson. I got mad at her and I told her I've got nothin' more to say to her unless she can find a better way to speak to me. I just don't need that shit.

"All her mother thinks I want is some pussy. Shit, man, I don't want any pussy! I've had my pussy and I can see what it got me. No, man, what I want is some attention, someone to say, 'How was your day today?' when I get home from work. No, I don't want any pussy. I just want some companionship and some human comfort. Ever since Claude Sterling was born, Sherelle's been all wrapped up with him and all her girl friends bein' around, and her mother sayin' I can't come by the house no more. It's hard, I tell you! I got some needs in all this, too. I need Sherelle to help me out, to talk to me, to listen to me, to share with me my thoughts and feelings. But I want things such so's she's not doin' things for me that, you know, I could be doin' for myself. I love my boy and there's probably nothin' I wouldn't do for him and Sherelle.

He hesitates for a second. "No, make that I *know* there's nothin' I wouldn't do for them two. My baby won't want for anything.

"What I'm tryin' to say is that I work hard and bust my ass and I'm responsible, and the last thing I need is to be left out of the center of attention. I want to be at the center with Sherelle and Claude Sterling, to have them close, to have that . . . that . . . stable family. That's it, a stable family. I want a stable relationship with Sherelle and I want a stable relationship with my son. As I see it, he's the only child I'm gonna have and I want to enjoy him thoroughly, man, and I want to teach him things about the world. It's ins and outs, you know."

He throws another stone. "But I have to learn them for myself first, but at the same time I still want him to know that I'm there for him and I'll be there to help open up the world for him. I need to show him, not simply tell him.

"Like take reading, for example. The first day of school he won't know how to read, but if I'm there for him I can help him with that. And with football, too. If his father was there with him showin' him how, he'd feel as if he was better at it. Wouldn't you? Same thing with fightin'. I've got a lot I can teach my son. 'Cause the father's the stable one in the family, at least he should be.

"You know that tattoo I got on my arm," Larry says as he takes off his jacket and rolls up his sleeve. His heart-shaped tattoo reads: L + S + CS. "See this? I had it put on a while back to prove to Sherelle my commitment to her and the baby. I'm glad I did it, too, man. I think it really showed her I care. But, you know there are days I wake up feeling that what I'm working for don't matter to her at all. I just wind up staying in bed with my funk. I need my family, man. Without that kind of responsibility I can't be strong. The more responsibility I have, the stronger I really feel. Now, I'm not sayin' I should be bitin' off more than I can chew, but I need some definite stable responsibility to feel connected. Man, without that it's back to no man's land and the four walls in my room. And that ain't no where.

"Do you realize how many teenage fathers are out there in the streets? She could've ended up with any one of those no-good bums. I mean, they ain't 'no good' or anything like that really, they're just bein' young. And, shit, we are young! And that's what I forget sometimes. It's just that I'm trying to act up to my responsibilities, my adult responsibilities, mind you, sort of before my time. But that's just the thing; it *is* my time whether I'm ready or not 'cause I am a father and I have a son."

Larry takes a deep breath. "It can really be a consuming trip, man. Anyways, like I was saying, Sherelle could have ended up with a dude who said, 'fuck this babe, that kid ain't mine,' or 'hell if you try to pin that rap on me.' You know what I mean?

"I could be just like them, and don't think I don't feel like runnin' and slidin' with the guys sometimes," he says with a crack of a smile on the side of his mouth. "You can even take this partner of mine, he's about the most conscientious teen father I know. He visits his little family all the time. But he don't think to bring a box of diapers or a carton of milk or something. He's got the right idea but he's still young. I ain't asking much, am I? I just want to be appreciated and be a part of their lives.

"This one's sort of crazy, ain't it? I mean usually it's the guy who dumps the girl after she gets pregnant or gives birth. He simply abandons her with all the work and responsibility for taking care of the baby. No wonder so many of these girls around here don't want to get married. They don't trust men. In some cases I can't blame 'em either. Sherelle's mother, for example. Part of her trip about having Sherelle stay away from me is that she herself got pregnant with Sherelle when she was sixteen, just like Sherelle, and her husband ended up leaving her. So she thinks the same thing's gonna happen to her daughter, that I'm gonna make all sorts of promises and then split up when I get tired of it, leaving Sherelle with Claude Sterling and God knows what other kids.

"But the straight-up truth is that, that ain't nothin' but out and out discrimination and we got laws against that, don't we? I mean, you can't discriminate against a person because of his race or religion or background *or* his sex! Yeah, that's what this scene is all about, I'm being discriminated against because I'm a man!'' he screams into the wind. "It's a fuckin' myth that the teen father is the villain, he's a victim in this thing like everybody else!"

"And your fight with Sherelle?" I ask. "Are you the villain or victim there?"

"Sharp question. I'm both, man, villain and victim. I know I shouldn't a gone off on her the way I did. I got no excuses. It was a bad play. I had actually come by that day feelin' pretty good and I just wanted to talk with her. But she wouldn't talk, not inside or outside on the street. And she was makin' me look the fool in front of her friends and everybody. It was the straw that cracked this camel's back. I just wanted a little attention from her, man. I actually don't remember some of what happened 'cause I was so angry. I lose all sense of values when I go wild, I forgot almost everything. It's like something gets snipped in my brain and I lose consciousness. Guess that's why they call it 'blind rage.' I lose sight of everything.

"I remember getting her to eventually step outside with me 'cause I didn't want to cause no scene up inside the center. You know, fighting in the center just isn't cool with Ed. And I lost it, man, just fuckin' lost it and went off and punched her right out, bam, right in the jaw. I swear I didn't know what I was doin'; just thinking of hittin' that girl makes me feel real sick. But I did it, and smacked her around a bit, too. Her friends pulled her away and Ed grabbed me. I think I even took a swing at him. I really don't know what I was doin'.

"And was I cussin'! Words even you probably don't

know. As I look at it, Ed was real smart, man. He took me cut back in the alley holding me and talking to me. I was so damn angry at her and at myself for hitting that woman I was crying, real hard, too. Hadn't done that in a long time.

"And, it didn't take long before the ol' grapevine caught up with her mother. The ol' babe called the police on me. They had a fuckin' warrant out for my arrest. Can you dig that? She was gonna have me arrested and thrown in jail! Good thing Ed was there, man, or I might have gone after her, too. He drove me down to the station and had me turn myself in before they actually caught up with me. Sherelle and her mother were down there waitin' for me. Heavy drama, man. Heavy drama of a tall order. Sherelle was pleadin' with her mother not to press charges against me. She really came through for me and I'll always appreciate her for that. I know I was out of my mind for swinging at her; I guess the pressure was just too much."

Larry stops. He lights a cigarette and pushes the sand into a small mountain with his foot. His shoelaces are still untied.

"I had a feeling something like that would happen," Larry says, looking down at the sand. "Sometimes I'd have this way of pickin' on her as soon as I'd see her. Right away I'd start in, tellin' her how she ought to do things and such. I know as I'm doin' it, I'm pickin' on her 'cause I'm angry 'cause she's not gonna pay enough attention to me. I imagine we both have some serious changes to go through.

"But I know I won't let these changes affect anything with my relationship with my son. No way. He means too much to me. Like financially, for example. I've set up this savings account for him that Sherelle handles. She's a dynamite saver, man, much better than me. I set it up so both our signatures are needed in order to write a check. That's to keep me from spending any of the money we've saved up, 'cause I love to make and spend money. No doubt about it. But I've known how to handle money for a long time, now, Dan, and big money at that."

"For a long time?" I challenge. "You're only sixteen."

"Man, there's a lot you've got to learn about bein' young and bein' in the streets. Around when I was eleven or twelve or so I knew I was hungry to learn about the world. I had met this pimp and he saw I was real quick and real intelligent. So he gave me five hundred dollars to see if I could do something with it. I turned it into twelve hundred bucks in six months, paying him back just like we'd said. I learned all about investing."

"In what?" I ask somewhat naively.

"In reefer, man. This pimp had taught me the ways of money, how to make it, how to turn it over quick. He's the cat who turned me on to bonds and interest-earning bank accounts. I still do a little business on my own. The assets from that pay for all our present expenses and my paycheck goes non-stop to our little savings account for Claude Sterling's future. Got to be thinkin' about planning for the future.

"When I was younger I dealt all kinds of junk; cocaine, heroine, speed, barbituates, dope, you name it. And it's been a stable head that's kept me away from all that stuff, except for a little reefer. But I know I need to become more stable in the future. You know, more relaxed, more in control of things; a more flexible person," he says as he bobs his head from side to side, "in the way I deal with things. More able to let things roll and slide off and shake off 'cause it wouldn't matter to me. And that takes some discipline, which I feel I don't have enough of right now, and it's something I want to show my son how to get for himself.

"You know," he says, as if he has just remembered something, "I know my mother taught me about responsibility and trust, but I could never tell her that 'cause, well, you know. I got to appear like I learned it on my own.

"And my father. I learned about moderation from him." His voice has a tone of endearment in it. "On the Thursday before he died he took me out with him. I'll never forget it. I was fourteen, almost fifteen then. I remember how glad I was to be out with the ol' man. I still have the bottle of Christian Brothers we drank that night. It's on a shelf in my room. I got so sick, man; that wine was wicked. But he taught me, in his own way, not to overdo things, especially with drugs and alcohol 'cause they can really make you sick. It sure made him sick. A few days later he was dead, man. Cirrhosis of the liver."

He pauses and lights another cigarette. The smoke from the match vanishes in the wind. He takes a long drag, letting the smoke drift out of his mouth and into the air.

"And that's my deep fear, man, that, without that stable family relationship, with me a strong father, my son will grow up like me when I was a kid; all wild and unruly, feeling uncomfortable, and hating and being a fighter. I really want something different for my son. I want him to have all the advantages I never had.

"I was never really close with my father. He moved out when I was a kid. He was an alcoholic, man, and a drug addict, too. He did some good things, though in his life. He wasn't all the way tripped out. He helped bring some dynamite job programs to Evanston. Headed up the whole thing. Not bad for an alcoholic and drug addict. Only around the time when he died did he start talkin' to me more. Maybe it was 'cause he knew he was dyin'. He use to tell me, 'If I die, not to feel bad and be sorry 'cause I lived a full life, I did all I wanted to do.' "

"Did his words help you out at all?"

"No, not really," he confesses with a smile. "No, I was really sad for sure. I just wished I knew him better. We never talked much, you know, like he never sat down with me and told me his whole life story or nothin'. But when we did talk, man, it was good. The thing is, Dan, we were gettin' a lot closer around the time he died. He had a beautiful life philosophy. He'd traveled all over the world, too. Been to all kinds places. He was in the Navy, maybe even in Korea.

"The man had him some strong arms, too. I once walked by the kitchen and saw him sittin' there at the table. He didn't see me, but I watched him shoot up. Man, right before my eyes. I'll never forget it; rolling up his sleeve, heating up his spoon, tying up his arm and then lettin' go with the junk right into his veins. Boy, did his muscles flex. I told myself I'd never ever mess with it."

Larry takes a final drag from his cigarette and tosses

it into the water. We retrace our steps through the sand and then along the streets and sidewalks toward Our Place. We continue to talk, but my attention is else-where. I keep hearing a conversation I had with his mother back in the spring when I first met Larry. I had called him on the phone to schedule a meeting. Mrs. Hobbs answered the phone in a friendly manner.

"No. Larry's not home now. He went to work this morning to fill in for a friend. He probably forgot you were going to call," she said in a motherly fashion.

"He's a busy man," I replied.

"No," she insisted, "he's a busy *boy*. He thinks he's a busy man, but he's not. He's still a boy."

And what have I heard out there on the lake's shore? Who is he who has spoken to me all afternoon? A boy? A man?

We stop our walk in the alley behind Our Place. It has been a long afternoon. Larry stands at a distance. "I'm bothered," he says, "about this book you're writing. It's just got to reach the kids, my peers; but they're not the kind who are gonna read this sort of thing. You know I want to help and if my story can help some kid somewhere I'll be happy. If it works, that'd be great. But I don't think it will. The ones I'm thinkin' need to be reached don't come around Our Place. They don't know Ed and they don't know what can be done at a place like this."

He takes a few steps toward me. Somewhere a car's horn is blasting. Somewhere a dog keeps barking. "It's just gotta reach the kids," he pleads. "It's just gotta reach the kids."

Afterword

It has been three years since I began to hear these stories, stories that reveal hard truths and rough realities. But these portraits, by their very nature, are incomplete, just as the lives of these young people are incomplete. It is too soon to know what course the life each of these teens will take. Prediction is, after all, the Achilles' heel of social science.

In the autumn, Rochelle Lawson will attend a college nursing program. Valerie Wallace and her son have left Evanston to live with her grandmother in Mississippi, where Valerie goes to high school. Janice Franklin, alias "Cookie," now works for an Evanston-based social service agency. Gwen White and her younger sister will attend the same western Illinois college in the fall, where they will share an apartment in the parents' housing complex and the parenting responsibilities for Gwen's two daughters. Joanne Johnson still lives in Alabama with her brother and her daughter, Renee. Jeanne Hutton has not returned to high school. Instead she works full time at an unemployment office. Larry Hobbs, too, has not returned to school. He continues to work long hours at Evanston Hospital.

And what of the others? Many feel battered by a society they experience as indifferent and insensitive, if not hostile, to their needs. Jobs for youths are scarce, as are opportunities for reliable and inexpensive day care. All feel the constraints of limited emotional and physical energy in meeting the demands of parental responsibility.

At Our Place, the teens have found in the adults a source of encouragement in an environment that helps them to build on their individual strengths. Our Place is where young people can work through the maze of their feelings and clarify their goals. The staff sees *living persons*, not abstract social categories.

In these stories, the teens describe a range of feelings and experiences that transcend their Evanston neighborhoods. These young voices—proud, frightened, innocent, bold, and tender—speak of courage and sadness and hope. They speak of the human capacity to endure pain and hardship with strength, determination, and resilience.

Pauline Thompson, the senior Partner, reminds us that all need not be determined by the tumult of teenage parenthood. She has emerged from this rough rite of passage with tenacity, direction, and commitment. Someone heard Pauline, and her account tells of the value and urgency of adults listening to the thoughts and feelings of young people. Her story illustrates what is possible: a life cared for and attended to by empathetic adults can achieve fulfillment of previously untapped potential.

Larry Hobbs is right. There is no time to waste.